The Finer Optic

THE FINER OPTIC

The Aesthetic of Particularity in Victorian Poetry

Carol T. Christ

Yale University Press   New Haven and London   1975

Designed by John O. C. McCrillis
and set in Baskerville type.
Printed in the United States of America by
The Vail-Ballou Press, Binghamton, N.Y.

Published in Great Britain, Europe, and Africa by
Yale University Press, Ltd., London.
Distributed in Latin America by Kaiman & Polon,
Inc., New York City; in Australasia and Southeast
Asia by John Wiley & Sons Australasia Pty. Ltd.,
Sydney; in India by UBS Publishers' Distributors Pvt.,
Ltd., Delhi; in Japan by John Weatherhill, Inc., Tokyo.

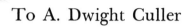

To A. Dwight Culler

Contents

Preface

Most attempts to establish the unity of Victorian poetry and poetics have dealt with moral and theological issues—the crisis of faith, the impulse to preserve disintegrating moral and religious values through literature. Frequently using Arnold's analysis of literature and culture as a touchstone, they have emphasized the moral function of art and the social role of the poet. But Arnold was in many ways a reactionary trying to restore a neoclassic objectivity and universality to modern literature. Coexisting with Arnold, and in fact creating much of his fear of the modern, is a preoccupation in Victorian poetry with the particular and the subjective. The Arnoldian emphasis of much Victorian criticism has obscured this preoccupation and with it the continuity between Victorian and modern literature. Figures as diverse as Tennyson, the Pre-Raphaelites, Browning, and Hopkins are united in a common concern with the particular that extends from the use of detail in their poetry to the epistemological issues it implies. Tennyson's microscopic eye, the Pre-Raphaelite fidelity to minute detail, Browning's dramatic monologues, and Hopkins's vision of a world of inscape and instress all reveal an interest not in those characteristics of nature immediately representative of the universal but in the immediately and peculiarly individual. Tennyson, Rossetti, Browning, Hopkins reverse Samuel Johnson's instruction to the poet; they do not remark general properties and large appearances but number the streaks of the tulip and describe the different shades in the verdure of the forest. Consequently, they face in their poetry, in a far more difficult way than earlier poets, the problem of transcending the particular. This preoccupation with the particular in Victorian poetry and the attempt to transcend it are the concern of the following pages.

ix

This book was originally a dissertation written under the direction of A. Dwight Culler. To him I owe my greatest debt. He first suggested that I think about the subject of particularity in Victorian literature and gave me invaluable help and encouragement while I was writing my dissertation. It would never have taken the form it did were it not for him. I would like to thank Zelda Boyd, whose enthusiasm about the manuscript made me return to it. Our discovery that we thought similarly about Victorian literature led to many conversations that have influenced my ideas. I would also like to thank Ulrich Knoepflmacher, who painstakingly read and commented upon every page of this manuscript, and Masao Miyoshi, who suggested several ways in which I could extend its focus. I am grateful to Larry Sklute, who read and commented upon the manuscript in its several versions and for whom no question about it was too large or too small. I wish to thank my editor, Catherine Iino, who did her work splendidly. Finally, I would like to thank Janet Buck, who first inspired me to study Victorian literature and who gave me many ideas and most of my enthusiasms.

The Finer Optic

For the philosopher, setting down with thorny argument the bare rule, is so hard of utterance and so misty to be conceived, that one that hath no other guide but him shall wade in him till he be old, before he shall find sufficient cause to be honest. For his knowledge standeth so upon the abstract and general, that happy is that man who may understand him, and more happy that can apply what he doth understand. On the other side, the historian, wanting the precept, is so tied, not to what should be but to what is, to the particular truth of things and not to the general reason of things, that his example draweth no necessary consequence, and therefore a less fruitful doctrine.

Now doth the peerless poet perform both; for whatsoever the philosopher saith should be done, he giveth a perfect picture of it in some one by whom he presupposeth it was done, so as he coupleth the general notion with the particular example.

Sir Philip Sidney, DEFENCE OF POESY

Introduction

Literary theorists from classical times to the present day have asserted that poetry contains a peculiar union of the universal and the particular. Aristotle's doctrine of mimesis taken together with his statement that poetry is more philosophic than history because "its statements are of the nature rather of universals, whereas those of history are singulars"[1] suggests such a union, and critics as distant in time and aesthetic orientation as Philip Sidney, Samuel Johnson, Samuel Coleridge, John Crowe Ransom, and William Wimsatt have been involved in elucidating literature's combination of the general and the particular.[2]

Within this agreement that literature contains some combination of generality and particularity, however, there has been much debate about the relationship and the proportion between the two. In *Rasselas* Samuel Johnson asserts that the business of a poet is to examine

> not the individual, but the species; to remark general properties and large appearances: he does not number the streaks of the tulip, or describe the different shades in the verdure of the forest. He is to exhibit in his portraits of nature such prominent and striking features, as recal the original to every mind; and must neglect the minuter discriminations, which one may have remarked, and another have neglected, for those characteristiks which are alike obvious to vigilance and carelessness.[3]

Johnson is typical of neoclassic critics in his assertion that the poet must disregard particularities in order to rise to "general and transcendental truths, which will always be the same." Many modern critics, on the other hand, tend to stress art's

1

particularity rather than its generality. Henri Bergson writes
that

> art always aims at what is *individual*. What the artist fixes
> on his canvas is something he has seen at a certain spot,
> on a certain day, at a certain hour, with a colouring that
> will never be seen again. What the poet sings of is a
> certain mood which was his, and his alone, and which
> will never return.[4]

To be sure, the issue in this debate is not a choice between
the general and the particular. Those critics who urge artists
to pursue the universal do not wish an art of abstract generality that avoids images; the very act of imaginative representation involves the selection of particulars. Rousseau
explains this paradox in his *Discourse on the Origin and
Foundations of Inequality*.

> Every general idea is purely intellectual; if imagination
> is in the least involved, the idea immediately becomes
> particular. Try to draw for yourself the image of a tree
> in general, you will never succeed in doing it; despite
> yourself it must be seen small or large, sparse or leafy,
> light or dark; and if it were up to you to see in it only
> what is found in every tree, this image would no longer
> resemble a tree. Purely abstract beings are seen in the
> same way, or are conceived only through discourse. The
> definition of the triangle alone gives you the true idea
> of it: as soon as you imagine one in your mind, it is a
> given triangle and not another, and you cannot avoid
> making its lines perceptible or its plane colored.[5]

Rousseau's statement implies that the only literature that does
not contain particulars is literature which consists in only the
abstract discussion of ideas. Once representation is involved in
artistic creation, the artist is not dealing with an abstraction
but with an individual. He is not saying man, but this man.
And once an artist has chosen to represent this character, this
action, this situation, this setting, he must choose particulars,

or specific attributes, that separate his subject from others of
the same class. Neoclassic critics debate not the exclusion or
inclusion of particulars per se but the grounds for the selection of particulars. In the passage above, Johnson does not
talk about the suppression of all particulars but about the
selection of striking and characteristic particulars that recall
the universal to every mind, and Pope states in the postscript
to his translation of the *Odyssey,* "The question is, how far
a poet, in pursuing the description or image of an action, can
attach himself to little circumstances without vulgarity or
trifling? What particulars are proper, and enliven the image?
Or what are impertinent, and clog it?" [6]

Similarly, although Bergson states that the situation which
the artist represents is uniquely particular, he goes on to explain that the audience's response to this particular situation
is general, and that this general response constitutes art's universality. Bergson is typical of many modern writers in his
location of art's universality in the response of the audience
rather than in the typicality of its subject. It is no longer the
blackbird itself which conveys the universal but the thirteen
ways of looking at it. This difference in understanding the
relationship of art's particularity and universality results both
from the disintegration of the idea of type in the modern
world and from the change, which had its origins in the
Romantic movement, from an emphasis on the object portrayed to one on the mind in the process of perception.
Writers previous to the nineteenth century for the most part
assume a Platonic view of the universe, according to which
universality is implicit in the characteristics of the object
portrayed. Writers of the nineteenth and twentieth centuries,
on the other hand, often do not assume the necessary typicality of objects of the same class, often doubt the very idea of
class except as an artificial construct, and find universality
in the play of the imagination upon particular subjects. They
see universals implicit not in the objects of perception but in
the categories of perception, in imaginative activity. The ways
in which writers understand this imaginative activity differ

greatly. George Eliot, for example, implies in her novels it
is the power of moral sympathy that gives universal meaning
to particular subjects. Wallace Stevens sees the mind's construction of a reality as the power that transforms particulars
into universals. Imagist poets find universality merely in the
aesthetic enjoyment of a sensuous image. No matter how differently writers locate and define art's universality, however,
there is no writer I know who asserts that art has no universality, for, as Bergson states, "this would no longer be communicating something, it would not be writing." [7] In fact, all
literature has a kind of universality just in its use of a vocab-
ulary and a syntax that are general and categorical by nature.
In addition, our expectation that art communicates experiences in some way significant of a general truth tends to
transform a particular, once set within the context of a work
of art, into an image. As W. H. Auden writes in the poem
"New Year Letter:"

> Though their particulars are those
> That each particular artist knows,
> Unique events that once took place
> Within a unique time and space,
> In the new field they occupy,
> The unique serves to typify,
> Becomes, though still particular,
> An algebraic formula,
> An abstract model of events
> Derived from dead experiments,
> And each life must itself decide
> To what and how it be applied.[8]

Thus we can see that the issue in the arguments about art's
universality or particularity is not the choice between abstract
universals or concrete particulars but the definition of the
dynamic between the two. Critics question not whether literature should contain detail but what the significance of
detail should be, and consequently what the criteria for its
selection are. They question not whether literature is exclu-

sively general or exclusively particular but in what way and to what extent particulars imply universals.

These aesthetic questions of course imply a larger philosophical issue concerning the relationship of the perceptible world to universal terms. An aesthetic that stresses art's generality assumes a Platonic view of the universe, in which things denoted by a common term have a similarity that implies a universal meaning, an eternal outline, or a necessary formula behind all of its concrete manifestations. In an essay written for the *Idler* on painting's need to suppress the particular, Joshua Reynolds asserts that "every species of the animal as well as the vegetable creation may be said to have a fixed or determinate form, towards which Nature is continually inclining." [9] For Reynolds, this form is more real than any of its specific representations. The aim of the artist, therefore, is to portray this fixed or determinate form, and in order to do this, he must select details to be as clearly characteristic and as purely ideal as possible. Each individual tulip in Dr. Johnson's garden suggests the definitive and perfect image of a tulip. The aim of art is to evoke this perfect image as powerfully as possible. To do so, the artist must suppress not all the particulars of the tulip, but those particulars which are accidental or peculiar, which do not definitively suggest the ideal tulip. The artist must distinguish not the general from the particular but the essential particular from the accidental particular.

An aesthetic that stresses art's particularity, on the other hand, usually does not assume that things denoted by a common name are essentially similar, but infers only an approximate or nominal universality, finding the essence of each thing in its individuality. Because such an aesthetic sees truth in the particular experiences of individuals in specific situations, all details that in any way characterize the subject are significant. Accidental particulars are essential particulars, and the writer consequently gives them an emphasis Johnson would have judged distracting and irrelevant.

This emphasis on art's particularity is a modern develop-

ment. Despite the discussion of the importance and function
of particulars throughout the history of criticism, not until the
eighteenth century was the assumption challenged that the
subjects of literature were essentially ideal and that its details
consequently represented general truths. During the eighteenth century, however, the novel, the emerging sensitivity
to the picturesque, and, later, Romanticism, all questioned in
various ways the neoclassic understanding of art's universality
and gave a greater importance to the particular than neoclassic aesthetics allowed. By the Victorian period, the sense
of the particularity of experience and the disintegration of belief in the reality of universals had increased to such an extent
that poets were forced to develop new aesthetics to deal with
this particularity and its relationship to art's universality.

To understand how the Victorians dealt with this problem
we must look briefly at the problem's history in eighteenth-
and early nineteenth-century aesthetics. Most Augustan art
attempts to portray ideal universals, images that suggest general and eternal truths. This insistence upon representing
general truths, which we can see in works such as the *Essay
on Man,* the *Essay on Criticism,* and "The Vanity of Human
Wishes," rests on a belief that nature operates by a permanent
set of universal laws applicable to all men. For the Augustans,
nature is "one *clear, unchang'd,* and *Universal* Light." The
directive for artists to "follow NATURE" means to discover
those laws by which she operates and to portray them in as
general a form as possible in order to be recognizable to all.
Because the Augustans understand nature principally as a
world order or a set of universal standards, their ideal of
truth to nature involves the conception of situations in clearly
general terms. Again, this means not that the artist must reject images completely for general philosophical precepts but
that the images artists use must be sharply representative in a
way that immediately places them and reveals their significance for us.[10]

For many neoclassical artists, however, this ideal of univer-
sally representative images required an aggressive suppression

of particularity. In the third of the annual *Discourses* he wrote as President of the Royal Academy, Reynolds asserts that the whole beauty and grandeur of painting consists in "being able to get above all singular forms, local customs, particularities, and details of every kind,[11] and in an *Idler* essay, he states that the painter will "by regarding minute particularities, and accidental discriminations, deviate from the universal rule, and pollute his canvass with deformity." [12] The Earl of Shaftesbury writes that the painter and the poet "hate minuteness and are afraid of singularity, which would make their images or characters appear capricious and fantastical." [13] In his thirty-sixth *Rambler* essay, Johnson likewise states that "poetry cannot dwell upon the minuter distinctions by which one species differs from another without departing from that simplicity of grandeur which fills the imagination, nor dissect the latent qualities of things without losing its general power of gratifying every mind by recalling its conceptions." [14]

It has been suggested that the Augustan suppression of particularity springs from their effort to create art that evokes the sublime,[15] and the statements of Johnson and Reynolds quoted above certainly support this interpretation. The Augustans' sense of the universe was hierarchical; far from seeing "a World in a Grain of Sand and a Heaven in a Wild Flower," they felt that bringing the reader's attention to a wild flower or a grain of sand while he was looking at the heavens would destroy the sublimity of his impression. More fundamental to the Augustan distrust of particularity, however, is their identification of it with the accidental. In an art which seeks to portray the essential outlines of its subject, any attention given to the inessential, the accidental rather than the substantial, confuses and weakens that portrayal. The reason the Augustans felt the danger of the accidental in poetry so acutely is probably related to the emerging climate of realism during the eighteenth century. If the empirical psychology of Locke and Hobbes, the skepticism of Berkeley and Hume, and the emerging form of the novel did not directly help create a growing skepticism about the reality and the know-

ability of universals, they certainly reflected one.[16] This skepticism has important consequences for poetry because it calls
into question the neoclassic understanding of mimesis. Neoclassic art defines itself as mimetic; Johnson's Imlac bases his
statement of the poet's task on the metaphor of a portrait.
But the mimesis Imlac defines is an ideal mimesis, a portrait
painted like the portrait of Juno by Zeuxis of Heraclea, who
gathered together all the maidens of his town, chose the five
most beautiful, and painted the best features of each. Most
Augustan definitions of such an ideal concept of mimesis contain an implicit warning against another concept of mimesis
—the imitation of the accidental, the inessential, of nature not
as she should be but as she appears to the eye.

The novel, which was developing in the last half of the
eighteenth century, of course embodies this realistic concept
of mimesis, but at the same time there was developing a kind
of poetry that also manifested a greater valuation of the particular—the picturesque. Perhaps the defining characteristic
of the picturesque is an emphasis on the pleasures of vision
apart from any truth value they might contain. Because the
picturesque is thus more concerned with emotional affect than
with objective truth, it does not seek to suppress the particular
in service of the ideal, but to exploit it, to look for the for-
tunate *accidental* collection of parts in a scene or building
that creates a picturesque effect.[17] Thomson's *The Seasons* is
the most significant poetic example of the picturesque; it was
praised most frequently not for its universal truth but for
its exquisite particularity. Even Johnson praises Thomson, not
for exhibiting those characteristics of nature "which are alike
obvious to vigilance and carelessness," but for showing the
reader things he never saw before.[18] In a digression on *The
Seasons* in his book on Pope, Joseph Warton derives from the
poem a poetic stressing the value of particularity. After prais-
ing the truth to nature of the particularity of Thomson's description he states, in a reversal of the Aristotelian distinction
between poetry and history, that "a minute and particular
enumeration of circumstances judiciously selected, is what

chiefly discriminates poetry from history, and renders the former, for that reason, a more close and faithful representation of nature than the latter." [19]

In many of its characteristics, the picturesque anticipates Romantic poetry, but when we turn to the Romantic critics, we unexpectedly find them maintaining the neoclassic concept of the universal to a much greater extent than pre-Romantic writers. In the *Biographia* Coleridge asserts:

> I adopt with full faith the principle of Aristotle, that poetry is essentially *ideal,* that it avoids and excludes all *accident;* that its apparent individualities of rank, character, or occupation must be *representative* of a class; and that the *persons* of poetry must be clothed with *generic* attributes, with the *common* attributes of the class: not with such as one gifted individual might *possibly* possess, but such as from his situation it is most probable before-hand that he *would* possess. [20]

Wordsworth makes a similar statement about the ideal character of poetry in the preface to the second edition of the *Lyrical Ballads.*

> Aristotle, I have been told, has said, that Poetry is the most philosophic of all writing: it is so: its object is truth, not individual and local, but general and operative;
> . . . Poetry is the image of man and nature. [21]

What separates the Romantics from the neoclassic poets is their location of the source of the universal. They do not find the minute and the particular inconsistent with the sublime and the universal, but rather seek the sublime and the universal in the minute, in the common, in the particular. The revolutionary character of Wordsworth's preface does not consist in any argument against the neoclassic universal but in its finding those universals in "incidents and situations from common life." The real has become the ideal. In his criticism of Reynolds, Hazlitt asserts that "the greatest grandeur may coexist with the most perfect, nay with a microscopic accuracy of detail." [22] Blake wrote in the margins of his copy of Reynolds' *Discourses:* "This Man was Hired to Depress Art"; "To Generalize is to be an Idiot. To Particularize is the Alone Distinction of Merit—General Knowledges are those Knowledges that Idiots possess"; "Singular & Particular Detail is the Foundation of the Sublime." Unlike the Augustans, the Romantics try to see "a World in a Grain of Sand and a Heaven in a Wild Flower," Resolution and Independence in a leech gatherer and Truth and Beauty in a Grecian urn, the sublime in the minute and the universal in the particular.

The Romantics' location of the universal in the particular involves a very different sense of the relationship of the universal and the particular from the Augustans'. Particulars are not Platonic imitations of ideal forms, as they tended to be for the eighteenth century, but in themselves living symbols, participants in the universal. Nature is not an imperfect copy of a perfect original but the form in which the spirit of the universe manifests itself. Coleridge does not speak of the artist's representation of the universal through an abstraction of ideal particulars but of his imaginative understanding of the *natura naturans* beneath the *natura naturata,* which results in the interpenetration of the universal in the particular and the particular in the universal.[23] Coleridge explains this union in a passage on Shakespeare.

It is Shakespeare's peculiar excellence, that throughout the whole of his splendid picture gallery . . . we find individuality every where, mere portrait no where. In all his various characters, we still find ourselves communing with the same human nature, which is every where present as the vegetable sap in the branches, sprays, leaves, buds, blossoms, and fruits, their shapes, tastes, and odours. Speaking of the effect, i.e. his works themselves, we may define the excellence of *their* method as consisting in that just proportion, that union and interpenetration of the universal and the particular, which must ever pervade all works of decided genius and true science.[24]

The change the Romantics created in the understanding of the relationship between universal and particular is, however, a consequence of the far more fundamental and significant shift of focus from the object portrayed to the mind in the process of perception. This change results in making the movement of individual consciousness the subject of poetry. Wordsworth is obviously not interested in presenting the ideal portrait of a leech gatherer but in demonstrating the way the mind can renew itself from such a sight. The Romantic poets try to portray not the eternal order of nature independent of the perceiver, but the interaction between nature and the perceiver—the ways in which the individual mind apprehends, feels, assimilates, creates, and remembers. Coleridge asserts in the analysis of the universal and the particular quoted above that the universal is not implicit in the particular, but that the imagination can transform particular sense impressions into universals.

The importance of the individual imagination in Romantic poetry allows it to be far more particular than neoclassic aesthetics permitted. Imagery may become representative of experience rather than idea. Because the poet is more interested in portraying the movement of mind than the objective order of nature, detail and imagery need not necessarily signify some universal characteristic of the object portrayed but may only suggest some aspect of mental experience. Particulars need not represent objective universal characteristics of an object; they may represent merely a subjective individual impression of the poet. Furthermore, particular situations and the way they contribute to experience become much more important. This importance is reflected in the very concrete sense of location in time and space the Romantic poets often give their poems. Wordsworth begins "Tintern Abbey" with the inscription "Composed a few miles above Tintern Abbey, on revisiting the banks of the Wye during a tour, July 13, 1798," and Coleridge prefaces "This Lime-Tree Bower My Prison," with a short account of the friends' visit and the accident that inspired the poem. For Johnson the in-

formation these inscriptions give would be irrelevant, distracting, and limiting at the beginning of a major poem, but for
the Romantics, it singles out a movement of mind in a particular situation, at a particular time and place, as a significant subject for poetry. Moreover, the individual personality
of the poet becomes important, because he is no longer objectively portraying nature but laying bare the movement of
his own soul.

Because the Romantics believed in the universality of the
imagination, their creation of a poetry that portrays the movement of the individual mind resulted in a particularity with
a correspondent universality. The Victorians, however, gradually lost the Romantic assurance that there existed universal
correspondences among individual imaginations and between
the imagination and the sensible world. Therefore, Romantic
assumptions about poetry led to an acutely un-Romantic sense
of the particularity of experience when inherited by the
Victorians. For the Victorians, the egotistical sublime no
longer revealed the universal mind underlying all individual
imaginations but came to pose the threat of solipsism. The
descendants of Wordsworth's lyrics are Browning's dramatic
monologues. The poet himself can no longer speculate on his
God; he can only show the reader Bishop Blougram, Cleon,
and Caliban speculating on their particular gods. Keats's negative capability, the empathy with the particular that enabled
him by himself to experience all the existential possibilities of
the universe, allowed the Victorians only a sense of the infinite possibilities of isolation. The rich depiction of detail
in Keats's lyrics suggests the ability of the self to expand into
the world; Keatsian detail in the poems of Tennyson or the
Pre-Raphaelites more often signals obsessive contemplation by
a character fixated in some morbid emotion. Detail portrays
not the ardent expectancy of a Madeleine but the obsessive
grief of an Oenone, a Mariana, an Aloÿse, a Guenevere. Furthermore, the Victorians lost the transcendental sense of nature that allowed the Romantics to perceive significance in
the most minute grain of sand. They therefore gradually came

to perceive nature as a collection of disparate particular forms with nothing to offer but the experience of their own sensations. By the end of the century the faculty for truth was no longer, as it had been for Coleridge, the power of seeing the universal in the particular but, in the words of Pater, "a power of distinguishing and fixing delicate and fugitive detail" [25] merely for the sake of the experience itself.

Between Coleridge's idealism and Pater's cheerful relativism, however, came a period of agony and confusion. The Victorians felt at once a desperate pessimism based on the fear of precisely what Pater embraces—experience with no meaning beyond itself—and made an equally desperate attempt to find some universal significance in objects.[26] The search for an objective standard of truth, the attempt to see the object as it really is, that we find in Ruskin, in Arnold, in Carlyle, in Mill, stems from an assumption that subjectivity distorts, that there is a great danger that one might see the object as it really isn't. Both the growing conviction of the subjectivity of experience and the demand for scientific standards of truth resulted in a greater emphasis on the particular. On the one hand, the insistence upon a more and more minute observation of detail, such as we find in Ruskin's *Modern Painters* or in the paintings of the Pre-Raphaelite Brotherhood, seems almost a desperation in the face of the world of objects, a frantic attempt to amass and enumerate particulars in the hopes of ordering a world increasingly resistant to human control and intelligence. On the other hand, the frequent poetic portrayal of minute objects was used to suggest the peculiarity of an individual character's vision, as does the blue vein on the Madonna's breast that the bishop of Saint Praxed's church imagines so vividly or the shell that transfixes the hero of Tennyson's *Maud*. The observation of minute particulars thus comes to signify both the solipsism the Victorians feared and their last attempt to discover a universal order in the world of things.

The developing sense of the particularity both of individual perception and of sensible objects results in a different use of poetic detail. In much Victorian poetry and painting, detail becomes scientifically precise and minute, conspicuously particular. Not wildflowers, but asphodels, jacinth, and woodbine present themselves for our attention, and not as the way to heaven but merely for their own sake. Particulars are not representative of a moment of imaginative experience that becomes in some way universal, like Wordsworth's daffodils, but merely descriptive of a single moment of consciousness, which is portrayed for its own interest and which rarely leads to a statement of universal judgment.

In the following chapters I am going to deal with the ways the Victorian poets portray and attempt to resolve the problem of particularity, how they transform mere particulars from portents of disorder and alienation into an aesthetic value, the means of a new kind of vision. I will concentrate on Tennyson, Rossetti, Browning, and Hopkins, for their poetry illustrates the problem most definitively and completely, but I will range as broadly as the problem itself. Because I am primarily interested not in providing readings of the poets I have chosen but in showing how their works, different as they are, suggest a similar awareness of a common problem, I have chosen to organize my discussion not around the individual writers but around the problems I see as uniting their work and as helping create a distinctive Victorian aesthetic. The three problems on which I have chosen to concentrate are morbidity, the grotesque, and the good moment. Each is a central preoccupation of Victorian literature, each is accompanied by an extraordinary emphasis upon minute detail, and each, I feel, suggests an aspect of the problem that particularity posed to the Victorian imagination—morbidity, the dangers and the possibilities of sensation created by absorption in purely personal emotion; the grotesque, an awareness of the prevailing difference and oddity of the world's created forms; and the good moment, the possibilities and limits of vision in a world of mere particulars.

While writing these pages, I have often recalled Allen Ginsberg's lines, "What did I notice? Particulars! The / vision of the great One is myriad." I quote them here to prepare the reader for the many and sometimes contradictory manifestations the concept of particularity had for the Victorian world. Philosophical problems often lose their precision when they appear in the world of literature, but what they lose in philosophical precision they often gain in psychological complexity. This is the study of both an aesthetic problem and a psychological predicament. I have tried to translate terms from one realm to the other. Where I have failed, I would like to think the reason lies in precisely the Victorian problem— the artificiality of species and the independence of the particular.

1

The Microscopic Eye:
Particularity and Morbidity

One day while spending a month in Switzerland, Tennyson and a friend, the Reverend Stenton Eardley, were rambling over the mountains. Eardley saw Tennyson suddenly go down on his hands and knees and look intently at something in the grass. "Look here," he exclaimed, "I can see the colour of the flower through the creature's wings." The "creature" was a dragon fly; the flower, an Alpine rose.[1] Such acute sensitivity to delicate, minute natural detail became a legend in the poet's lifetime. It struck some answering enthusiasm in the Victorian public, and nature and Tennyson were, they found, the same. Mrs. Gaskell made the man in *Cranford* go back to look at some ash buds because Tennyson had said they were black, and an astronomer and his wife compiled a book attempting to describe the entire composition of the natural world from passages of Tennyson's poetry. The paintings of the Pre-Raphaelite Brotherhood, the writings of Ruskin, and even the poetry of Hopkins spring from a similar zeal for exact fidelity to natural detail. This fanatic concern for scientific accuracy, which made Tennyson keep charts of isothermals and isobars in his room to ensure the exactness of his scientific allusions and Holman Hunt go to the Dead Sea on the day of Atonement when painting *The Scapegoat* to make sure the light would be exactly as it had been on the day the goat was turned out of the temple, obviously results from the rising predominance of scientific views of truth in the Victorian period, but the extraordinary sensitivity to minutiae that always accompanies such accuracy is less easy to explain. Tennyson's famous vision of the moonlight reflected in a nightingale's eye as it was singing in a hedgerow or Millais's picture of Ophelia drowning amid flowers that dazzle the spectator stamen by stamen have a microscopic exactitude artificial to normal vision, almost as if a whole generation of artists were born nearsighted. This peculiar consciousness of the minute particulars of nature furthermore plays a paradoxical role in the work of these artists. Although they pursued the accurate observation of nature more zealously than any Romantic, they decreasingly felt any sympathetic power in nature. The uses of acute sensitivity to natural detail thus often become curiously detached from any interest in nature itself.

Tennyson was the first of the Victorian poets to show this sensitivity to detail. The descriptions in his poems are characterized by a remarkable visual precision. He notes the "lines of green that streak the white / Of the first snowdrop's inner leaves." In "The Bosky Brook," he describes the peculiar undergrowth of hemlocks and sallows. "Oenone" tells of the lizard that, "with his shadow on the stone, / Rests like a shadow." Despite the precision of such descriptions, however, they rarely obtrude themselves on the reader's attention with an insistence out of proportion with a sense of the whole. As you read about "that hair more black than ashbuds in the front of March," you only pause afterwards, if at all, to recollect whether ash buds are black in early March. But there are a few poems, atypical of most of Tennyson's poetry in their use of description, where detail does become the center of focus. In these poems Tennyson uses it to suggest a disturbed quality of perception, a sensitivity to sight and sound so intense and so emotionally charged that it must be called morbid. In "Mariana," for example, the details Tennyson uses have a profoundly unnatural quality to them; they stand out with an emphasis so precise it appears fantastic to normal vision.

> With blackest moss the flower-plots
> Were thickly crusted, one and all:

> The rusted nails fell from the knots
>   That held the pear to the gable-wall.
> The broken sheds looked sad and strange:
>   Unlifted was the clinking latch;
>   Weeded and worn the ancient thatch
> Upon the lonely moated grange.[2]

The striking characteristic of Tennyson's use of detail here is his distortion of natural focus. It is as if he collapses the distance between each object he contemplates and the beholder. He creates no sense of surrounding context or natural perspective but represents each object in the same intensity and detail. Objects therefore appear isolated, much like a series of disjunct, close-up, still photographs.

Most of the objects that compose the landscape of the poem—the ticking clock, the fly buzzing in the pane, the dust in the afternoon sunlight—are quite mundane; so mundane, in fact, that they usually even escape perception. The sharpness of their images therefore conveys a sensitivity morbid in its emotional intensity. Although the poem is not put in Mariana's mouth, the consistent emotional tone Tennyson gives the landscape makes us feel it is her perception of the house we are given. The way the landscape is seen thus becomes the means of approaching Mariana's sensibility. Mariana's obsession with her desertion keeps her fixated in a static emotional attitude that makes the slightest movement or sound strike her with extreme sharpness. The chirping of the sparrow, the ticking of the clock, the sound of the poplar all "confound her sense." Objects appear to her with an acuteness that mesmerizes her: she stares at the shadow of the poplar all night; she cannot stand to look at the dust in the afternoon sunbeam. The slightness of these impressions conveys the blankness of a mind that under prolonged emotional strain seizes upon any object to find some release. Only through the sensation of objects around her can Mariana escape her despair within. Yet the sharpness of the images shows this sensation is painful as well. Her impressions only afflict her with renewed consciousness of her own situation. The visual isolation of images from each other suggests her own isolation. The way the landscape continually reminds us of the passage of time—the heaven at morn and eventide, the cock crowing, the clock ticking, the dust in the afternoon sunbeam—tells us of Mariana's obsession with time and of her consciousness that her own life remains without hope of change. Not merely the objects of the language—the blackened sluice, the pear falling from the gable wall—but also the way those objects are presented—the minuteness, the sharpness, the isolation of the images—portrays Mariana's emotion. The poem presents not just a landscape but a peculiar mode of perceiving landscape.

Of course many of Tennyson's poems—"The Lotos Eaters," "The Lady of Shalott," "Oenone," "Tithonus," *Idylls of the King,* to name just a few—use landscape to portray emotion. In his review of Tennyson's first two volumes of poetry, John Stuart Mill praises Tennyson for his power "of *creating* scenery, in keeping with some state of human feeling; so fitted to it as to be the embodied symbol of it, and to summon up the state of feeling itself," and later defines Tennyson's style as "statuesque" rather than picturesque because the forms in his poetry are not of unequal degrees of definiteness, "but each individual object stands out in bold relief, with a clear decided outline." [3] "Mariana" is like much of Tennyson's poetry in these respects, but it is peculiar in its association of intense consciousness of minute detail with emotional isolation and madness.

We can see the distinctiveness of Tennyson's presentation of the landscape in "Mariana" by comparing it to its companion poem, "Mariana in the South." Tennyson got the idea for his southern Mariana while traveling through a barren stretch of country in the south of France. He determined to write a poem expressing the experience of desolate loneliness as it would exist under the influence of different sense impressions, but not only the geography changes in the second poem: Tennyson presents the landscape in a very different way. He does not give the reader a number of disjunct, highly particularized impressions of objects, but describes the landscape surrounding the house in an orderly and connected fashion.

> With one black shadow at its feet,
>   The house through all the level shines,
> Close-latticed to the brooding heat,
>   And silent in its dusty vines:
> A faint-blue ridge upon the right,
>   An empty river-bed before,
>   And shallows on a distant shore,
> In glaring sand and inlets bright.

By giving a clear sense of the area's geography and of open space extending to a horizon, the poem creates a feeling of objectivity and freedom of movement totally lacking in the earlier poem. Consequently, the impression of isolation and imprisonment here is much less powerful than it is in "Mariana." The different manipulation of detail in "Mariana in the South" fails to present the peculiar mode of perceiving landscape that reflects Mariana's emotional obsession.

Readers have noticed the recurrence of two states in Tennyson's poetry: trances in which the boundaries that delimit the identity of things melt away, as in the Prince's seizures in *The Princess* or Sir Percivale's hallucinations in *The Holy Grail,* and states in which detail appears with microscopic exactitude. Critics usually see this observation of detail as Tennyson's way of preventing the external world from losing identity and significance.[4] Intense awareness of detail, however, seems often to accompany these trancelike states. For example, in "Armageddon," a poem Tennyson wrote at about the age of fifteen and later adapted in "Timbuctoo," he describes a trance similar to ones he said he experienced as a boy.

> I felt my soul grow godlike, and my spirit
> With supernatural excitation bound
> Within me, and my mental eye grew large
> With such a vast circumference of thought,
> That, in my vanity, I seemed to stand

Upon the outward verge and bound alone
Of God's omniscience. Each failing sense,
As with a momentary flash of light,
Grew thrillingly distinct and keen. I saw
The smallest grain that dappled the dark Earth,
The indistinctest atom in deep air,
The Moon's white cities, and the opal width
Of her small, glowing lakes, her silver heights
Unvisited with dew of vagrant cloud,
And the unsounded, undescended depth
Of her black hollows. Nay—the hum of men
Or other things talking in unknown tongues,
And notes of busy Life in distant worlds,
Beat, like a far wave, on my anxious ear.

    I wondered with deep wonder at myself:
My mind seemed winged with knowledge and the strength
Of holy musings and immense Ideas,
Even to Infinitude. All sense of Time
And Being and Place was swallowed up and lost
Within a victory of boundless thought.
I was a part of the Unchangeable,
A scintillation of Eternal Mind,
Remixed and burning with its parent fire.
Yea! in that hour I could have fallen down
Before my own strong soul and worshipped it.

Here extraordinary sensitivity to detail is paradoxically one
of the characteristics of this trancelike state in which the poet
loses "all sense of Time / And Being and Place." Tennyson's
vision resembles the archetypal mystic vision of the One in the
Many. Blake's vision of "a World in a Grain of Sand" and
our contemporary poets' descriptions of drug experiences find
a similar euphoric sense of the unity of the world in an intense consciousness of particulars. Allen Ginsberg's poem,
"Wales Visitation," describes this experience in terms similar
to Tennyson's.

Stare close, no imperfection in the grass,
            each flower Buddha-eye, repeating the story,
                the myriad-formed soul
Kneel before the foxglove raising green buds, mauve bells
                                            drooped
        doubled down the stem trembling antennae,
    & look in the eyes of the branded lambs that stare
    breathing stockstill under dripping hawthorne—
    . . . .
What did I notice? Particulars! The
        vision of the great One is myriad [5]

Tennyson's description of this state is important for the
rest of his poetry, because of the awareness it reflects of the
way man's emotions shape his perception of the world's physiognomy. In the passage from "Armageddon," he emphasizes
not the spiritual paradox of the one in the many but the per-
ceptual paradox that an extreme emotion can create an extraordinary consciousness of particulars, whose individuality
is intensified rather than extinguished by the emotion. Extreme emotional states such as euphoria or morbidity often
transform our emotional reactions to the landscape. The
world seems one in its reflection of either abundance and
beauty or decay. The normal sense of boundaries between
objects thus can disappear, while any detail can carry the significance of the whole. The slighter the detail, in fact, the
more intensely it conveys the poet's consciousness of one spirit
animating the landscape.

A study of the psychology of obsession by Erwin Straus [6]
offers some interesting parallels to Tennyson's use of detail.
Straus shows that obsessions belong to the pathology of the
sympathetic relations that connect man with his world. The
obsessed experiences a disturbance in the usual balance between awareness of abundance and awareness of decay. He
sees only deterioration, deformation. The world loses its polar
articulations and seems unified in the emotion it reflects.
Straus contrasts the psychology of obsession to that of hashish

intoxication. For the person under the power of hashish, the world seems one in its reflection not of decay, but of beauty, harmony, and sympathy. There is at once a fading of boundaries between subject and object, a feeling of encompassing all time and space, and an increased consciousness of particularity. Straus quotes Baudelaire's "Le poème de haschisch" to illustrate this state but he could as well have used Tennyson's "Armageddon" or Ginsberg's "Wales Visitation." Behind his analysis of the psychology of both hashish intoxication and obsession is the assumption that there is no duality between our experience of self and our experience of the world, but that in one and the same act we experience both. Our sense of physiognomy of the world, even in the most fundamental categories of space and time, reflects our perception of ourselves.

In "Mariana" and "Armageddon," Tennyson shows an understanding of obsession remarkably similar to Straus's. The morbidity portrayed in "Mariana" can be seen as the inverse of the euphoria in "Armageddon," and the two use detail in similar ways. The world seems homogeneous to Mariana not in its beauty but in its isolation and disintegration. The recurrence of the refrain and the lack of progression in the poem's monotonous repeated movement from night to day, without hope of change, suggest this sameness. Because Mariana experiences only one emotion, the most insignifigant details convey that emotion and jump out before her sight with an extraordinary sharpness. The awareness of detail in the poem thus becomes symptomatic of the destruction of normal sympathetic relations with the world.

Tennyson felt that the reality of self was easier to grasp than the nature of matter.[7] "The Ancient Sage," in which he describes these trancelike states he had experienced as a boy and had depicted in Armageddon," testifies to this lifelong conviction. Even as early as *The Devil and the Lady,* a play written at the age of fourteen, we find Tennyson wondering whether the phenomenal world only gains existence by our consciousness of it.

O suns and spheres and stars and bolts and systems,
Are ye or are ye not?
Are ye realities or semblances
Of that which men call real?
. . . .
I have some doubt if ye exist when none
Are by to view ye; if your Being alone
Be in the mind and the intelligence
Of the created, should some great decree
Annihilate the sentient principle
Would or would ye not be non-existent?
'Tis a shrewd doubt.

[II.i.40–43, 51–57]

Tennyson's shrewd doubt suggests not only a belief that the
reality of the spiritual is greater than that of the material but
a psychological insight into the nature of perception. Spirit
shapes the landscape, giving it its peculiar kind of reality.
Many of Tennyson's most powerful poems present a morbid,
self-enclosed, isolated character. Mariana, Oenone, the lotos-
eaters, Fatima, Lucretius—the poems that portray these characters rarely contain sharply defined events or rhetorical
points. Rather, they try to let the reader inside an obsessive
emotional imprisonment that totally shapes the character's
environment and holds him static within it. One critic, Martin
Dodsworth, finds the most interesting element of such poems
in what they imply concerning the nature of reality. They
contain a constant confusion between the subjective and the
objective which calls into question the very nature of man's
relationship to the external world.[8] Tennyson's use of particularity also reflects the awareness Dodsworth describes, that
it is possible for the world to exist only as the materialization
of our subjectivity.

The Romantic poets too were concerned with the way the
external world reflects, symbolizes, and materializes subjectivity. Coleridge's "we receive but what we give" could well
describe Mariana and her landscape. What distinguishes Ten-

nyson from the Romantics, however, is his interest not in
the common interchange between self and world but in states
of extreme emotion, obsession, or hallucination, and their
effects on perception. Furthermore, he writes of such states
not in the lyric voice but through a dramatis persona, which
distances the emotion from the poet in making him the objective portrayer of a separate character's subjective emotion.
These changes show that Tennyson was less concerned with
the universal interdependence of self and nature than with
the way subjectivity can isolate and distort. As his insistence
upon scientific accuracy shows, Tennyson is at once more conscious of the objective reality of nature than the Romantics
and more concerned with the way in which not universal but
abnormal emotional states shape our experience of the landscape. His poetry suggests a separation similar to the one
Ruskin makes in his definition of the pathetic fallacy between
"the ordinary, proper, and true appearances of things" and
"the extraordinary or false appearances when we are under
the influences of emotion, or contemplative fancy." The madness of most of Tennyson's characters suggests that Tennyson,
like Ruskin, felt that indulgence in such influences of emotion
was morbid. For the Romantics, reality lies in the reciprocal
relationship between mind and nature. For Tennyson, objective reality and its subjective impression are separated in a
way they rarely are in Romantic poetry.

   Maud is Tennyson's most complete exploration of the subjectivity of perception and of the psychology of madness.
Tennyson said of *Maud* that "the peculiarity of this poem is
that different phases of passion in one person take the place
of different characters." [9] Its originality springs from its use
of disconnected lyrics, each of them conveying one of these
phases of passion Tennyson speaks of, to tell a rather long
and complex story. Events are presented through the medium
of the emotion they provoke. *Maud* thus reverses the normal
order of presentation of a long narrative poem: the structure
of emotions is the primary fact the poem gives us; we must
reconstruct from this the order of events. The very form of
the poem thus insists upon the primacy of perception.

The way the poem presents the phenomenal world also reflects that primacy. The landscape in the first part of the poem is overly brilliant, almost garishly colored.

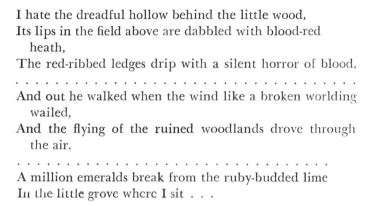

I hate the dreadful hollow behind the little wood,
Its lips in the field above are dabbled with blood-red
    heath,
The red-ribbed ledges drip with a silent horror of blood,
. . . .
And out he walked when the wind like a broken worlding
    wailed,
And the flying of the ruined woodlands drove through
    the air.
. . . .
A million emeralds break from the ruby-budded lime
In the little grove where I sit . . .

The exaggerated vividness of the landscape shows the hero hysterically, almost pathologically sensitive to his environment. External objects are constantly appropriated by the speaker and converted to emblems of his moods. As a result they lack a firm phenomenal existence.

After the speaker has killed Maud's brother, his sensitivity toward the landscape changes. He becomes acutely conscious of minute detail. He stares at the wild flower on the hill immediately after the murder; he notices a ring on the brother's finger as he lies dying; he becomes transfixed by a shell lying on the Breton shore. These objects maintain their identity in a much firmer way than did the landscape earlier in the poem. He does not give them the same exaggerated emotional coloring but becomes mesmerized by the objects in themselves. When we first see him in Brittany, to which he has fled after the murder, he is staring at a shell at his foot.

See what a lovely shell,
Small and pure as a pearl,
Lying close to my foot,
Frail, but a work divine,
Made so fairily well

> With delicate spire and whorl,
> How exquisitely minute,
> A miracle of design!

Despite the fact that the landscape lacks its previous emotional coloring, it still reflects the speaker's psychology. His sensitivity to detail at this point is a measure of his self-alienation. He has just committed a murder that has irrevocably separated him from the one person that he has learned to love, yet he is unable to fasten his mind on anything but trivial detail. He cannot directly confront the enormity of what he has done. Tennyson explicitly describes the psychology of this sensitivity to detail later in the lyric.

> Strange, that the mind, when fraught
> With a passion so intense
> One would think that it well
> Might drown all life in the eye,——
> That it should, by being so overwrought,
> Suddenly strike on a sharper sense
> For a shell, or a flower, little things
> Which else would have been past by!

Under the shock of extreme emotion, the mind reaches out for some object to occupy it. The strain of emotion produces the intense clarity of what are often trivial visual impressions. Oscar Wilde describes this psychological phenomenon in *The Picture of Dorian Gray*.

> The spray of lilac fell from his hand upon the gravel. A furry bee came and buzzed round it for a moment. Then it began to scramble all over the oval stellated globe of the tiny blossoms. He watched it with that strange interest in trivial things that we try to develop when things of high import make us afraid, or when we are stirred by some new emotion for which we cannot find expression, or when some thought that terrifies us lays sudden siege to the brain and calls on us to yield.[10]

The speaker's sensitivity to detail in *Maud* provides a similar key to his psychology. He reaches out for the shell to find some escape from the terrifying fact of what he has done. He tries to make it a symbol of himself in an oblique attempt to face his experience. Like the animal that once inhabited it, he tentatively pushed a foot into a very beautiful world, only to be pushed back into himself. Like the shell, he feels a fragility together with an indestructible core of self. Despite his attempts to identify himself with the shell, however, the disproportion between the reality of his situation and the mental event of seeing the shell is too great to carry the symbolic weight he tries to attach to it. Consequently, his vision of the shell comes to signify something quite different from his conscious formulation. The self-pity and minuteness of it show a desperate attempt to preserve some small core of self. The isolation and self-enclosedness of the shell suggest his isolation and self-alienation. His fixation upon the shell reflects the disintegration of order and loss of proportion, almost verging on madness, that the murder has created. In fact, when he eventually goes mad, he magnifies the sounds from the street outside the madhouse in a similar manner:

> And the hoofs of the horses beat, beat,
> The hoofs of the horses beat,
> Beat into my scalp and my brain,
> With never an end to the stream of passing feet.

This emphasis upon detail is very similar to that in the landscape of "Mariana." To be sure, the psychologies of the two characters differ somewhat. Mariana is imprisoned by an emotional obsession, which shapes her world in its own reflection. The hero of *Maud* is facing the disintegration of order under the weight of a catastrophic event. Nevertheless, the two poems use detail in a similar way. Both inflate minute objects so that they appear with a disproportionate emphasis and intensity, but their significance comes not from what the characters may see them as symbolizing but from the failure of perception this focus suggests. It becomes symptomatic of the loss of balance and proportion, of the inability to integrate and order experience, and of a consequent isolation in purely subjective perception.

The loss of the capacity to order experience according to traditional principles and the isolation in individual perception are precisely the perils that the Victorians feared and that the sensitivity to particularly in Victorian literature often reflects. A sensitivity to the microscopic comes to imply a particularistic conception of the universe, according to which each individual is a law only unto itself. The particular understood as the minute comes to connote the particular as the absolutely individual. John Fowles's recent novel, *The French Lieutenant's Woman* (Boston, 1969), contains an incident that illustrates the historical predicament. Charles, the novel's Victorian hero, is walking through the woods to a meeting with a fallen woman—the consequences of which will psychologically and philosophically alienate him from Victorian society. As he strides through the woods, he keeps thinking his mind should be occupied with gloomy moral precepts; instead he has a vision of the forest in brilliant particularity, which makes him realize his loss of any set of ordering generalizations in the face of a world whose every element is absolutely individual.

> The trees were dense with singing birds—blackcaps, whitethroats, thrushes, blackbirds, the cooing of wood-pigeons filling that windless dawn with the serenity of evening; yet without any of its sadness, its elegiac quality. Charles felt himself walking through the pages of a bestiary, and one of such beauty, such minute distinctness, that every leaf in it, each small bird, each song it uttered, came from a perfect world. He stopped a moment, so struck was he by this sense of an exquisitely particular universe, in which each was appointed, each unique. A tiny wren perched on top of a bramble not ten feet from him and trilled its violent song. He saw its glittering black eyes, the red and yellow of its song-gaped throat— a midget ball of feathers that yet managed to make itself the Announcing Angel of evolution: I am what I am, thou shalt not pass my being now . . .

It seemed to announce a far deeper and stranger reality than the pseudo-Linnaean one that Charles had sensed on the beach that earlier morning—perhaps nothing more original than a priority of existence over death, of the individual over the species, of ecology over classification. We take such priorities for granted today; and we cannot imagine the hostile implications to Charles of the obscure message the wren was announcing. For it was less a profounder reality he seemed to see than universal chaos, looming behind the fragile structure of human order.[11]

Like Charles, the Victorians experienced the collapse of many of the principles that had given their lives meaning. The ancient truths of religion, morality, philosophy, and politics were called into question one by one. This loss of belief left the Victorians with fragments of experience unordered by any principle. The accepted generalities were gradually dissolving, leaving nothing but a morass of disjunct particulars.

The codes that replaced the traditional schools of morality and religion all emphasized the importance of particulars. One of the most basic and revolutionary changes Darwin's concept of evolution brought about was the elimination of typological thinking. Darwin showed that there was no such thing as an immutable species, and with his demonstration came the collapse of the twin assumptions that a limited number of fixed, unchangeable "ideas" underlie observed variability and that reality inheres in the type, not in variations from the type. Now the variations, the uniquenesses, the particulars become the most important factors in natural processes, and the idea of species becomes an artificial abstraction. No two individuals are exactly the same, and the variations between them are what propel the process of natural change.

The theories of two other thinkers who helped undermine the premises of Victorian religious belief, Malthus and Bentham, also share this emphasis on the particular. Reality lies in the individuals that survive or the individual acts that result in happiness. There was also a great interest during the period in atomic theory. Not only did much chemical and physical research seem to point in the direction of atomism, but there was a fascination with Lucretius and his philosophy.[12] Tennyson wrote a poem about Lucretius, Arnold projected a poem about him and discussed his poetry as an example of the modern temperament in his essay "On the Modern Element in Literature," and H. A. J. Munro published one of the first modern critical editions of *De Rerum Natura* in 1860 and a translation in 1864. According to atomic theory, what appear as units to our senses are in fact collections of minute individual particles. The reality of the type was thus undergoing attacks by many different theories, all of which insisted upon a nominalistic universe without biological types and species, without a priori concepts, without general ethical imperatives.

The collapse of generality caused by the loss of religious belief and by contemporary political and scientific theories left the individual isolated in himself with no trustworthy guide to action. Conceiving of the universe as a mass of particulars led logically to seeing experience as wholly subjective and particular, which ultimately developed into solipsism. In *The Central Self*, Patricia Ball explores the difference between Romantic and Victorian attitudes toward self-consciousness. She concludes that what was for the Romantics a source of self-discovery became for the Victorians a burden that posed the threat of self-imprisonment.[13] This change in attitude results from the difference in the extent each felt it possible to generalize from personal experience. The Romantics believed that the truths they discovered could communicate certainty to others and could inspire all human enterprise. The Victorians lost this assurance, and self-consciousness consequently became a paralyzing disease, leading even to insanity or suicide. *Maud* describes this danger. For the hero of the poem, the codes and values of society have lost all meaning. His alienation from society and his obsession with its wrongs have

thrown him back completely into himself, but this isolation
has produced an introspective morbidity, a "hysterical mock-
disease," which threatens to destroy his sanity. Self-consciousness has become for him an imbalance of perception, an isolating sickness, which can only be cured through love of Maud
or reintegration with society. What he has lost, in a sense, is
the ability to feel himself part of a generalization. His refusal
"to take the print of the golden age" means also that he cannot feel himself a member of a community. From the point
of view of our own age, where social alienation is an accepted
and laudable stance, it is difficult to realize how extremely
painful it was for the early Victorians. The Victorians con-
sidered the dangers of social disaffection very great, at the
same time they felt their own alienation from the golden age
more strongly than ever before. In combining an unequivocal
condemnation of society with a picture of the terrifying psychological consequences such a rejection entails, *Maud* reflects
the poignancy of the Victorian predicament. The poem is
ultimately unable to resolve the dilemma. The hero chooses
social commitment in joining the army to fight the Crimean
War, but the only value his decision reveals is that of sanity
over insanity.

Maud was reportedly Tennyson's favorite poem and the one
he chose to recite most often when asked to read from his
works. Tennyson's affection for the poem suggests that he felt
the hero's dilemma quite keenly. In fact, the most important
advice he felt he could give a young man going off to the
university was to cast aside "all maudlin and introspective
morbidities." [14] And Tennyson is only one of several writers
of the period who associates self-consciousness with social
alienation and self-imprisonment and who sees in it a dangerous threat. In *Sartor Resartus,* Teufelsdröckh finds the cure
for his spiritual crisis, which is modeled on Carlyle's own, in
moving away from paralyzing self-consciousness toward useful
work and integration with society. In his essay "Characteristics" Carlyle asserts that self-consciousness is the disease
peculiar to the modern age. Matthew Arnold suppressed

"Empedocles on Etna" because of the unrelieved painfulness,
which he states resulted from Empedocles' isolation in his
self-consciousness with no vent for his suffering in action.
"The dialogue of the mind with itself," far from offering
exciting new possibilities of experience, becomes a prison
which isolates Empedocles on top of the mountain, Teufelsdröckh toiling along the Rue St. Thomas, and the hero of
Maud in an insane asylum.

In each of these works, the hero's self-consciousness is characterized by morbidity, by the loss of a sense of proportion
and order in an obsessive preoccupation with his feelings and
impressions. In the preface of 1853, Arnold proposes an aesthetic he hopes will act as an antidote for this state of mind
peculiarly endemic to the modern age. Both of the basic
principles on which this aesthetic is founded—that poetry
should try to represent great human actions that appeal most
powerfully to the elemental, permanent human affections, and
that poets should concentrate upon unity of structure in composing their works rather than individual beauties of expression—are reactions to the problem of particularity. The first
is an attempt to escape the predicament of Empedocles, which
derives, Arnold sees, from the Romantic belief that "a true
allegory of the state of one's own mind" is the highest goal
art can pursue. When the mind becomes isolated in dialogue
with itself the artist is left to represent the particular subjectivity of an Empedocles. Arnold sees this as drastically reducing literature's objectivity and universality. In reaction he
proposes what is in effect an aesthetic of generality, whereby
the artist seeks out the greatest human actions that appeal to
the most universal human passions. Only by transcending the
particular, the subjective, and the exclusively modern can literature regain its ancient objectivity and power. To the failure to transcend the particular Arnold also related the
problem of style. Those poets who concentrate on expression
rather than action diffuse the focus of a work of art by attend-
ing to separate thoughts and images rather than the total
unity. Although at first glance this appears to be merely a

sound principle of poetic construction, Arnold implies by it
much more. In a letter to Clough, he decries the influence of
Keats on English poetry and sees Browning unfortunately developing in the same direction. Both poets, he feels, do not
understand "that they must begin with an Idea of the world
in order not to be prevailed over by the world's multitudinousness." [15] For Arnold, preoccupation with style implies an
excessive contemplation of particulars, which results not just
in artistic disunity but in a collapse of metaphysical order.
Culture and Anarchy portrays Arnold's fear of that collapse.
The work seems propelled by a horror of fragmentation, of
the mere particular as a governing force, and by a desperate
search for a single unifying principle to which all action and
phenomena can be related—culture, perfection, sweetness,
light, Hebraism, Hellenism. "Doing as one likes," depending
solely on the particular as a motive for action, leads to anarchy and the dissolution of moral and social order.

Arnold thus reveals the problems particularity suggested to
the Victorian imagination. Unlike the poetic theorists of the
eighteenth century, those of the nineteenth century who proposed an aesthetic of generality did so in reaction and defense
against those problems. Both the kind of poetry Arnold tried
to write and his decision to give up writing poetry in order
to seek general ethical and cultural imperatives represent a
different answer to the threat of a particularistic universe
from those of the poets I am considering. In his book on Victorian poetic theory, Alba Warren argues that Victorian class-
icism sprang not from an assurance of order but from the
Romantic conviction that the times were diseased.[16] We can
certainly see this conviction in Arnold. Cardinal Newman,
too, bears out Warren's argument. He asserts that poetry
should strive to represent the ideal, to delineate the perfection
the imagination suggests, in order to bound and confine the
confused luxuriance of real nature and thus provide a purity
and truth the world refuses to give.[17] Even when these men
assert positions similar to those of Reynolds and Johnson,
they felt the possibility of order breaking down, of particular-

ity asserting itself, much more acutely than did eighteenth-
century writers.

In the *Essay on Man,* Pope asks:

> Why has not Man a microscopic eye?
> For this plain reason, Man is not a Fly.
> Say what the use, were finer optics giv'n,
> T'inspect a mite, not comprehend the heav'n?
> Or touch, if tremblingly alive all o'er,
> To smart and agonize at ev'ry pore?
> Or quick effluvia darting thro' the brain,
> Die of a rose in aromatic pain?

The situations in which Tennyson uses abnormal sensitivity
to particularity suggest that he feels it implies a loss, similar
to the one Pope describes, of the sense of proportion that
enables man to comprehend his relationship to the universe.
Like Arnold, Tennyson fears that the microscopic eye, the
power to inspect a mite, does indeed result in failure to
prehend the heaven. Pope goes on to explain, however, that
this loss of proportion creates an intensity of feeling that is
unbearably painful, while Tennyson values the intensity of
feeling he gains in his microscopic eye. His use of particularity suggests not only a loss of order but a new interest in
the possibilities of emotion and sensation. Admittedly, his
attitude toward these possibilities is ambivalent. The characters who feel so intensely in Tennyson's poetry also totter on
the verge of madness; he obviously felt their intensity was
morbid and dangerous. But he returns to such characters
again and again, showing a fascination with intensities of
emotion and sensation that will be the central preoccupation
of much poetry later in the century. Though he is a reluctant
revolutionary, he is a genuine one. The next two sections of
this chapter, on Rossetti's poetry and on the paintings of the
Pre-Raphaelite Brotherhood, will show how the use of detail
to portray intense emotion in Tennyson's poetry anticipates
the central concerns of the Pre-Raphaelite movement.

Much of the change in sensibility that distinguishes the middle from the early Victorian period can be seen in the relationship of the Pre-Raphaelites to Tennyson. They were fascinated by Tennyson's early poetry. Its sensuousness, its medievalism, its morbidity powerfully stimulated their imaginations: Rossetti and Millais both painted Marianas, the Pre-Raphaelites all contributed to Moxon's illustrated Tennyson, and Holman Hunt did a large oil of the Lady of Shalott. But in all their Tennysonian works, they made subtle changes in the values attached to Tennyson's symbols. They upset the delicate balance of fascination and withdrawal that is Tennyson's response to absorption in personal or aesthetic emotion and sought out this absorption wholeheartedly. Tennyson went to the land of the Lotos but returned; the Pre-Raphaelites forgot all thoughts of home and stayed.

Perhaps with the different value the Pre-Raphaelites attached to absorption in intense emotion, my terms should change. What Tennyson saw as morbidity, the Pre-Raphaelites were to seek out as a kind of sensationalism. But I retain the term morbidity to suggest the connection between them and Tennyson. Even if they did not see their art as morbid, their Victorian critics certainly did, and Tennyson's preoccupation with morbidity shows the new kind of interest in perception the Pre-Raphaelites were to further develop.

Just as in their painting the Pre-Raphaelites were drawn to Tennysonian subjects, so in his poetry Rossetti often treats situations similar to Tennyson's. Like Tennyson, he was fascinated with states of intense emotion, and like him again, he often uses an abnormal sensitivity to detail as a means of portraying such states. "The Bride's Prelude," for example, one of Rossetti's earliest poems, centers upon a very Tennysonian situation. Aloÿse, a deserted maiden obsessed with her betrayal and guilt, could well become an archetypal Tennysonian woman who lives imprisoned in some emotional obsession, like Mariana or Oenone. Yet Rossetti handles the situation very differently. He presents not only Aloÿse's point

of view but also that of her younger sister Amelotte, so that
the poem shows us not a timeless, changeless, totally exclusive
emotional imprisonment, but a crisis point where we see both
Aloÿse's reluctant recital of her past and Amelotte's sense of
dread in hearing her sister's story.

Rossetti uses an intense sensitivity to detail to convey Amelotte's state of mind in listening to her sister.

> Although the lattice had dropped loose,
>   There was no wind; the heat
> Being so at rest that Amelotte
> Heard far beneath the plunge and float
> Of a hound swimming in the moat.
>
> Some minutes since, two rooks had toiled
>   Home to the nests that crowned
> Ancestral ash-trees. Through the glare
> Beating again, they seemed to tear
> With that thick caw the woof o' the air.
>
> But else, 'twas at the dead of noon
>   Absolute silence; all,
> From the raised bridge and guarded sconce
> To green-clad places of pleasaùnce
> Where the long lake was white with swans.
>
> Amelotte spoke not any word
>   Nor moved she once; but felt
> Between her hands in narrow space
> Hew own hot breath upon her face,
> And kept in silence the same place.[18]

Insignificant details that usually pass unnoticed—the splash
of the hound plunging into the moat, the cry of the rooks
flying through the air, her own breath against her face—strike
Amelotte's sense with a new violence. Her emotional state
resembles the one Aloÿse describes when she first becomes
sick.

Motion, like feeling, grew intense;
Sight was a haunting evidence
And sound a pang that snatched the sense.

The intensity with which sense impressions strike Amelotte
reflects the tension of her mind in trying to assimilate the
experience she is having. Her effort to understand what her
sister is saying, her dread of it, the disintegration of her
former consciousness of things all make her senses extraordi-
narily receptive to any stimulus. The sharpness of the impressions of slight details conveys the terrible tension of her
mind to the reader.

Rossetti, like Tennyson, thus turns sensitivity to natural
detail to expressionistic uses. He portrays the way emotion
can change our sense of the landscape, can make us perceive
it in its particularity or its vagueness, or can cast strange
meanings over the details of everyday life. Michael Rossetti
once said his brother cared little for descriptive poetry because
it exhibits and extols objects instead of turning them into
"the medium of exchange between the material world and
the soul." [19] In other words, Rossetti is interested not in nature but in the way our vision of the landscape reflects our
subjectivity.

Despite his concentration on the way psychology shapes our
sense of the external world, the details in Rossetti's poetry
remain remarkably superfluous. What strikes us about the details of which Amelotte is so acutely conscious in the passage
quoted above is their lack of resonance or symbolic depth.
Although there is a sense of violation in the cry of the rook
Amelotte hears, much like the violation of her sense of innocence, the cry never really attains the depth of a symbol.
The details of the passage have an irrelevance, almost a ran-
domness, about them which keeps them from being absorbed
into Amelotte's consciousness. This differs considerably from
Tennyson's use of detail. In "Mariana," for example, emotion
so fills the details of the landscape that we lose a firm sense

of their phenomenal existence. The details in Rossetti's poems, on the other hand, have a much firmer location in time and space. The following stanzas, for example, describe the room in which the two sisters are sitting immediately before Aloÿse begins her story.

> She paused then, weary, with dry lips
>   Apart. From the outside
> By fits there boomed a dull report
> From where i' the hanging tennis-court
> The bridegroom's retinue made sport.
>
> The room lay still in dusty glare,
>   Having no sound through it
> Except the chirp of a caged bird
> That came and ceased: and if she stirred,
> Amelotte's raiment could be heard.

The unnatural clarity of slight sounds—the tennis game, the chirp of the bird, the rustling of Amelotte's dress—conveys the silence and tension in the room. The separate mention of each item extends our sense of the duration of the moment before Aloÿse speaks just as the tension of the moment extends it for the two girls. Occasionally an image seems to tremble on the brink of symbolic signification. The caged bird, for example, could suggest Aloÿse's situation. But if images portend meaning, that meaning is rarely developed. This failure to develop images into a symbolic pattern gives the poem a shallowness of surface in which objects have a purely phenomenal existence. Images function not to explore the meaning of the sisters' experience but to extend the sense of time and psychological tension before Aloÿse begins her story.

In his essay on Rossetti, Pater praises Rossetti for trying to create in his poetry "an exact equivalent to those data within." His praise defines Rossetti's artistic ideal. In much of his early poetry, Rossetti strives to attain a minute realism of perception and sensation. He tries to capture the way stimuli first hit the mind, before going through any process of assimilation toward meaning. The shallowness of surface I have described in "The Bride's Prelude" keeps the focus of the poem on what Pater calls "pure perception." [20] The purely phenomenal existence of objects ensures a constant awareness of each moment's location in time and space. The mention of sounds creates an almost physical feeling of time passing from moment to moment. Rossetti uses the sounds to convey not only the progression of time, however, but the sisters' experience of it. The slightness of sense impressions and the large amount of space between them slow the movement of the poem in a way that portrays the sisters' intense consciousness of the present and their dread of the future. Thus, through his use of detail Rossetti creates a tension between the elongation of time the sisters feel and its constant movement forward toward Aloÿse's revelation, which conveys the moment-to-moment process and sensation of psychological change with a radical realism.

"My Sister's Sleep," a poem written at about the same time, also uses acute sensitivity to detail to portray a state of intense emotion. A young man and his mother have been sitting up a number of nights to watch over a sick sister. Rossetti describes the room as it looks to the boy.

> Through the small room, with subtle sound
>   Of flame, by vents the fireshine drove
>   And reddened. In its dim alcove
> The mirror shed a clearness round.
>
> I had been sitting up some nights,
>   And my tired mind felt weak and blank;
>   Like a sharp strengthening wine it drank
> The stillness and the broken lights.
>
> Twelve struck. That sound, by dwindling years
>   Heard in each hour, crept off; and then
>   The ruffled silence spread again,
> Like water that a pebble stirs.
>
> Our mother rose from where she sat:
>   Her needles, as she laid them down,

Met lightly, and her silken gown
Settled: no other noise than that.

'Glory unto the Newly Born!'
    So, as said angels, she did say;
    Because we were in Christmas Day,
Though it would still be long till morn.

Just then in the room over us
    There was a pushing back of chairs,
    As some who had sat unawares
So, late, now heard the hour, and rose.

Here the details have a clearness and a bareness that deny
any meaning but their sensation. They totally resist symbolic
interpretation. Yet Rossetti places these details in the religious
context of the coming of Christmas morning and the sister's
death. The pushing back of chairs in the room overhead, for
example, is merely an incidental sound from another room
that might have disturbed the sister's sleep, but it coincides
exactly with the coming of Christmas morning and the discovery of her death. Most readers of the poem have seen this
combination as an example of the flabbiness of Rossetti's
poetic technique,[21] but one critic, Jerome McGann, argues
that by making the sensory details resist explication in terms
of the religious experience, yet occupy at least as emphatic a
place, Rossetti creates a deliberate tension between the religious and sensory experiences of the poem that forces us to
see the importance of the pure and nonsymbolic detail.[22] The
details become almost antisymbols in the aggressiveness with
which they resist interpretation.

    In his definition of the pathetic fallacy in *Modern Painters*,
Ruskin asserts that the highest order of poet does not let human emotion color the facts of the external world, but keeps
subject and object distinct, making sure, even in the midst
of powerful emotion, "to keep his eyes fixed firmly on the *pure
fact*." [23] In maintaining a separation between human emotion
and the objects of the landscape, Rossetti creates a poetic

technique that suggests Ruskin's ideal. The change in poetry and in philosophy that Rossetti's technique and Ruskin's criticism imply is a significant one. To see the attribution of emotion to the environment as a fallacy, one must have discarded the Romantic sense of the correspondence between the realm of human experience and the realm of nature. Because the Victorians no longer feel a correspondent breeze within, they see correspondence between man and nature as false. In her book *The Pathetic Fallacy in the Nineteenth Century* Josephine Miles analyzes poetic vocabularies through the century to demonstrate a change in poetry from a focus on objects as associates of human emotions to a focus on the perceived qualities of objects.[24] This change in focus obviously reflects a change in belief, a gradual separation between the order of man and the order of nature. The focus upon sensed qualities reaches its height in Pater's impressionism, which I shall discuss in a later chapter. Here I shall only note that the gradual separation of subject and object and the growth toward impressionism is one of the ways in which Victorian poetry anticipates modern literature. Imagist poetry, for example, and its ideal of precisely visualizing concrete impressions, or, to choose a more recent example, the nouveau roman, whose aim Robbe-Grillet describes as making objects refuse signification and establish themselves only by their phenomenal presence,[25] both imply a belief, which Rossetti's poetry anticipates, that the only meaning objects offer is the mere fact of their sensation.

I do not mean to imply that Rossetti sees the sole end of poetry as the representation of mere sensation. Despite its use of detail, "My Sister's Sleep" does not deny the meaning of the religious experience it portrays but forces upon us a new perspective toward it. We see it as it is experienced together with all the concrete sensuous impressions, irrelevant in a traditional sense, that accompany it. In his essay on the metaphysical poets, T. S. Eliot asserts that the mark of a poet's mind is the ability to amalgamate disparate experiences which for the ordinary man have nothing to do with each other.

The poet reads Spinoza, falls in love, hears the noise of a typewriter, and smells the cooking in the next room, and unites these experiences to form new wholes. Eliot feels that poets since the seventeenth century have lost this ability, but as Rosamond Tuve argues, the ideal he describes, psychological realism as a sufficient end of poetry, is essentially a modern, not a Renaissance ideal.[26] In creating a poetry whose unity is based on perception rather than idea, Rossetti anticipates this development in modern poetry. He attempts to show experience as it presents itself to consciousness, in all its apparent disunity, and to form a new kind of poetic unity based on perception.

We can thus see from Rossetti's poetry that although he at first seems to have preoccupations similar to Tennyson's he builds from them in very different ways. Both poets were fascinated with morbid and obsessive states of emotion, one of whose symptoms was an extreme and distorted sensitivity to detail. Tennyson sees such states as having a timeless, changeless, totally self-enclosing quality, which shows the threat of self-imprisonment they posed for him. Rossetti explores the relation between perception and morbid emotion in a much more neutral way. He emphasizes the medium of time in which the processes of perception and feeling take place. The crucial role time plays in his poetry shows how much greater the possibilities of movement and change are in his poetic world, possibilities that remove the threatening element Tennyson attaches to states of morbid emotion. The protagonists of both poets reflect the change between the two. Tennyson's morbid characters—Mariana, the hero of *Maud*, Oenone—are permanently alienated; they live "without hope of change." Rossetti's characters—Amelotte, the speaker of "My Sister's Sleep"—are more often possessed by a temporary state of strong emotion. His poems, much like "Mariana," contain a strong sense of the prolongation of time; nevertheless, his characters are experiencing some crisis point of change. While morbid emotion and the consciousness of particularity it entails shows a singularity of perception, they involve not the threat of permanent imprisonment but a new awareness that can be freely explored.

Rossetti's unqualified acceptance of absorption in strong emotion signifies a great change in the role of the artist in society. Rossetti himself provides an allegory for this change in his prose tale, "Hand and Soul." The tale describes the career of Chiaro, a medieval Italian artist. One day while looking out his window, Chiaro sees a bloody battle taking place in front of his great fresco *Peace*. Seeing the painting streaked with blood at the end of the battle, Chiaro despairs of his attempt to teach his generation by painting myths of faith. He then has a vision of a beautiful woman, who tells him to paint only his soul. Tennyson resembles the earlier Chiaro; he feels a vocation to be a social poet. One of the prevailing themes of Tennyson's poetry is the danger of isolation in private emotion and the virtue of social commitment. Rossetti, on the other hand, sees only Chiaro's vision of the woman telling him to paint his own soul. He is an intensely private poet, oblivious of any social role. In fact his strongest values, intense emotion and pure perception, are those later to become the foundation of the aesthetic movement. Tennyson's characters are socially alienated; Rossetti himself is. His alienation results in a more radically subjective poetic voice, in which he explores the processes of emotion and perception for their own sakes.

Nowhere does Rossetti assert the value of pure perception more clearly than in "The Woodspurge." In this lyric, the poet, distressed by some unnamed grief, walks out at random, following the wind. When the wind falls still, he sits down, drops his head between his knees, and looks at the ground.

> My eyes, wide open, had the run
> Of some ten weeds to fix upon;
> Among those few, out of the sun,
> The woodspurge flowered, three cups in one.
>
> From perfect grief there need not be
> Wisdom or even memory:

> One thing then learnt remains to me,——
> The woodspurge has a cup of three.

The only thing the poet has and gives the reader is the simple sight of the woodspurge. Rossetti does not assert any symbolic or intellectual content to his vision. If the fact that the woodspurge has "three cups in one" seems to suggest the trinity, the poem is conspicuous in its failure to develop that implication—almost as if Rossetti is suggesting the religious allusion only to deny it, to transform it into a mere visible fact. Yet the memory of that fact is indelible, and simply in itself offers the poet a possibility of renewal. The way the poem is written reflects the value placed on perception. It offers no prior history or setting, no explanation for the poet's grief, but merely records his actions and sensations in the simplest possible terms.

"The Woodspurge" reflects the distance Rossetti has traveled from the Romantics. Blake wanted to find "Heaven in a Wild Flower," and Wordsworth found proof of Peter Bell's moral insensitivity in the fact that "A primrose by a river's brim / A yellow primrose was to him / And it was nothing more." Although the Romantics started with the particular, they wanted to transcend it by discovering in it the symbol of a general truth. Even Tennyson has this desire, although he has more difficulty in understanding the meanings his symbols carry. He is sure his flower in the crannied wall would provide the clue to "what God and man is" if he could only discover it. Rossetti, however, insists on the fact that a woodspurge is a three-cupped woodspurge, and it is nothing more. Rossetti again recalls Ruskin's poetic ideal. Using the passage from "Peter Bell" I quoted, Ruskin distinguishes three ranks of men:

> the man who perceives rightly, because he does not feel, and to whom the primrose is very accurately the primrose, because he does not love it. Then, secondly, the man who perceives wrongly, because he feels, and to whom the primrose is anything else than a primrose: a star, or a

sun, or a fairy's shield, or a forsaken maiden. And then, lastly, there is the man who perceives rightly in spite of his feelings, and to whom the primrose is for ever nothing else than itself—a little flower apprehended in the very plain and leafy fact of it, whatever and how many soever the associations and passions may be that crowd around it.[27]

Ruskin feels that the best poets belong to this third class of men, and certainly "The Woodspurge" demonstrates just such a separation between the very plain and leafy fact of a plant and the human emotion associated with it.

But despite the fact that Rossetti's poetry and Ruskin's criticism reflect a similar sense of the separation between human emotion and natural objects, Rossetti and Ruskin pursue this separation for different ends. Ruskin urges poets to avoid the pathetic fallacy, so as to attain both truth to nature and an emotional containment that he feels necessary for moral strength. The separation between natural facts and human emotions in Rossetti's poetry, on the other hand, results from his attempt to portray the act of perception in its most immediate and elementary form. In her essay "Against Interpretation," Susan Sontag asserts that criticism should not interpret the work of art to show what it means but describe it in all its sensuous immediacy to show how it is.[28] Rossetti is against interpretation of natural objects for a similar reason. He does not attempt to convert them into emblems of general truths. Rather, he tries to portray the sensuous immediacy of a particular moment of perception.

Rossetti's effort to attain a sensuous immediacy in art often brought him into a position subversive to Victorian art and morality. Nowhere is this more evident than in "The Blessed Damozel." The subject of the poem is a conventional one: the mutual longing for reunion of an earthly lover and a dead and emparadised lady. The extraordinary element of the poem that stirred controversy both then and now is the image of the blessed damozel. Pater remarked of the poem that one of

its peculiarities "was a definiteness of sensible imagery, which
seemed grotesque to some, and was strange, above all, in a
theme so profoundly visionary." [29] Indeed, the poem presents
the blessed damozel with a startling combination of religious
iconography and distinct sensuous detail.

> The blessed damozel leaned out
> From the gold bar of Heaven;
> Her eyes were deeper than the depth
> Of waters stilled at even;
> She had three lilies in her hand,
> And the stars in her hair were seven.
>
> Her robe, ungirt from clasp to hem,
> No wrought flowers did adorn,
> But a white rose of Mary's gift
> For service meetly worn;
> Her hair that lay along her back
> Was yellow like ripe corn.
>
> . . . .
> And still she bowed herself and stooped
> Out of the circling charm;
> Until her bosom must have made
> The bar she leaned on warm,
> And the lilies lay as if asleep
> Along her bended arm.

The sensuous details of these stanzas have a realistic particularity that makes them jump out of the religious iconograph-
ical context. By using sensuous imagery in such a visionary
theme, Rossetti cannot help but affect how we see the traditional religious symbols. The blessed damozel's breast making
the gold bar of heaven warm turns the gold bar of heaven, a
clichéd symbol like "pearly gates" or "golden streets," into a
concrete physical object. The image of her hair lying along
her back like ripe corn gives a physical presence to her beauty
that causes us to sense the religious symbols that adorn her—
the three lilies, the seven stars, the white rose—as physical ob-

jects. She seems to be a Pre-Raphaelite "stunner" artfully posed in an angel's costume. Rossetti empties the symbols of their traditional religious meaning by making them so startlingly physical.

By making religious emblems an adornment and aspect of the damozel's physicality, Rossetti creates in the image itself a fusion of the holy and the sensuous. The traditional religious connotations of the symbols give the blessed damozel a sacred value, but this value is redefined in sensuous terms. She thus becomes an image of the sacredness of the human union of spiritual and physical love. Her image anticipates the lyric she sings later in the poem in which she imagines how heaven, when her lover arrives, will become merely the setting in which the two will realize their earthly love. Heaven centers upon them, not they upon God, and all its possibilities are turned to use in the fuller realization of their love. The poem redefines the holy, and it is through his manipulation of detail that Rossetti creates a symbol for his redefinition in the blessed damozel.

By interpreting the poem in this way, however, I am in a sense undermining its use of detail. The poem aggressively insists that an image is a particular sensuous presence not reducible to its signification. By using details like the damozel's yellow hair with an intensity and clarity far greater than that of anything else in the picture, Rossetti makes them stand out with a hypnotic sensuous presence not integrated with the whole. Susan Sontag declares in her essay that "in place of a hermeneutics we need an erotics of art." [30] "The Blessed Damozel" says much the same thing. It implies that the only way to imagine an object is as a particular physical presence. The relation between the soul and the material world is sensation, and because sensation must be of particulars, this view of the relation necessarily implies a nominalistic view of the world. It thus rejects generality for particularity as our mode of knowledge.

Rossetti's nominalism undermined many Victorian aesthetic assumptions. The principal Victorian critics—Carlyle, Arnold,

Ruskin—prized art's ability to show us truth and to present great ideas. The emphasis of their poetic theories was almost entirely on art as statement. They were preoccupied with the content, the meaning, the practical ends of poetry. As a result of their moral aesthetic, directed so strongly toward content, they intensely distrusted the sensuous medium of art. Any affirmation of its independent value implied a trust in sense, which they saw as undermining both morality and reason. Rossetti's insistence upon its value thus seemed to endanger both moral principle and intellectual knowledge. Although Robert Buchanan's infamous essay, "The Fleshly School of Poetry," certainly contains a warped view of Rossetti's poetry, it shows very clearly the ways Rossetti's aesthetic threatened these Victorian values. "To aver that poetic expression is greater than poetic thought" means "by inference that the body is greater than the soul, and sound superior to sense." [31] The Victorians wanted to look at the palace of art only from the outside. When Rossetti tried to live in it, they condemned him for his fleshliness. Because of its assertion of the sensuous value of the image, "The Blessed Damozel" was both morally and aesthetically subversive, and it was through the particular that Rossetti accomplished his subversion.

In "The Card Dealer," Rossetti makes the subversiveness of his use of the image implicit by associating it with a seductive and sinister woman. The poem describes a painting by Theodore von Holst of a beautiful woman, richly dressed, who is sitting at a lamp-lit table dealing cards, with a peculiar fixedness of expression. The symbolic significance of the poem is difficult to determine. Rossetti once said the woman represented intellectual enjoyment,[32] but the poem does not support this interpretation. The speaker comes to see her as something closer to fate or life, yet even this interpretation is strangely detached from the sheer fascination the image holds for him. The details of his description of the painting are much more convincing than any of his speculations upon its meaning. Here, for example, is an image of the lights reflected onto the cards from the woman's rings:

> Her fingers let them softly through,
>   Smooth polished silent things;
> And each one as it falls reflects
>   In swift light-shadowings,
> Blood-red and purple, green and blue,
>   The great eyes of her rings.

The unnatural clarity of this slight detail conveys an almost hypnotic fascination with the image itself that transcends any of his later attempts to affix a meaning to it. The way the woman draws the viewer into her game gives the image a seductively sinister quality, which springs not from whatever meaning she has but from the sensuous power of the image. Many of Rossetti's poems associate a beautiful and evil woman with an art object holding magic powers. Rose Mary and her beryl stone, Sister Helen and her wax doll, Helen of Troy and the cup in the shape of her breast—all suggest Rossetti's vision of art as a necessarily erotic experience. Just as in Rossetti's view of love souls can know souls only through bodies, so in art the sensation of the image is an essential and self-sufficient part of our understanding of it.

Rossetti's insistence upon the value of sensation and his attempt to make art mirror its processes had little to do with any interest in the external world. Nature frankly bored him. "D. G. Rossetti," wrote his sister Christina, "shuns the vulgar optic." What did interest him were just those introspective morbidities Tennyson warned upstanding young men to cast aside. Rossetti was not an upstanding young man in Victorian eyes, and he was certainly the lesser poet, but the shift of value is nonetheless significant. Rossetti glorifies intensity of sensation; he wants to "smart and agonize at ev'ry pore," to "die of a rose in aromatic pain." His preoccupation with extreme emotion and minute movements of perception may still strike us as morbid, but he luxuriates in his own morbidity.

In addition to using the particular in poetry, Rossetti helped begin a movement toward particularity in painting.

Hunt, Millais, and Rossetti first banded together to form the
Pre-Raphaelite Brotherhood in revolt against the academic
art of their day, which was largely based on the teachings of
Sir Joshua Reynolds. One of the basic principles of "Sir
Sloshua," as they called him, was that art should avoid particularities and details of every kind in order to create ideal
forms more perfect than any actuality. The Pre-Raphaelites
vigorously rejected his idea that art should represent generalizations and insisted that the artist should go directly to
nature, "rejecting nothing, selecting nothing, and scorning
nothing." The Pre-Raphaelites found support for their doctrine of truth to nature in Ruskin, who was just as vehement
as they were in his rejection of Reynolds' artistic neo-Plato-
nism. The highest art, according to Ruskin, is that which contains the most truth to nature, and truth to nature demands
not getting above particular forms, but showing the specific
character of every kind of rock, every class of earth, every form
of cloud, every species of herb and flower.

The Pre-Raphaelites pursued their doctrine of truth to
nature by a fanatic insistence upon absolute accuracy in the
slightest detail. Millais looked all over London for a car-
penter to serve as the model for the figure of Joseph in *Christ
in the House of His Parents,* in order to get the development
of the muscles just right. Holman Hunt spent weeks on the
shore of the Dead Sea, a rifle over his knees as protection
against bandits and wild animals, to paint the landscape for
The Scapegoat with absolute accuracy. To paint *The Eve of
St. Agnes* Millais posed his wife in the bedroom of James I at
Knole on a freezing winter night, and when he found out the
moonlight was not strong enough to shine through the stained
glass and throw warm gules on Madeleine's fair breast, he
rushed back to London to get a bullseye lantern, indignantly
insisting Keats was wrong. The Pre-Raphaelites worshipped
the vulgar optic to the point of self-parody.

Through a combination of laziness, lack of skill, and the
discovery of his personal artistic bent, Rossetti gradually
drifted away from the original principles and members of the

brotherhood. In later life, he took pains to dissociate his aesthetic from theirs, insisting that his works did not bear any resemblance to Hunt's and that the brotherhood was merely the result of "the visionary vanities of half-a-dozen boys." [33] The extreme stylization, the absorption of detail into decorative motif, and the concentration on medieval and mythical subjects of Rossetti's later work separate it from that of the naturalistic Pre-Raphaelites—Hunt, the early Millais, Ford Madox Brown, Arthur Hughes, and their imitators. Even in Rossetti's earliest paintings, such as *The Annunciation* or *The Girlhood of Mary Virgin,* the pale color, the idealized figures, and the lack of detail show how little he was interested in courting Hunt's and Millais's nature. Typically, he painted the lily in *The Annunciation* from an artificial flower. He never completed the one picture, *Found,* in which by painting a wall brick by brick he made a desultory attempt to justify his Pre-Raphaelite credentials. Because Rossetti's paintings do not show the sensitivity to detail that those of the other artists do, I will deal only with their paintings here.

Hunt bitterly resented what he saw as Rossetti's apostasy. Not only, according to Hunt, did Rossetti betray the original principles of the movement, but by his greater notoriety, he clouded the public's conception of true Pre-Raphaelitism. The contradictions in their articulated theories, however, make the impulses behind the art of Rossetti and the naturalistic Pre-Raphaelites seem much more distant than they actually are. Despite the fanatic adherence of the Pre-Raphaelites to the doctrine of truth to nature, their pictures most often strike us with their lack of realism. Pound once described a Pre-Raphaelite painter who in preparation for painting a twilight scene rowed across the river in daytime to see the shape of the leaves on the further bank, which he then drew in full detail.[34] Pound's satire points to the unnaturalness of painting each object, no matter how near or far, how central or insignificant, with the same microscopic clarity. Not only is this uniform clarity of detail across the total field of vision untrue to the way we see, but it constantly distracts our attention from the main subjects of the pictures. When we look at a painting such as Hunt's *The Awakened Conscience,* whose subject is the sudden moral awakening of a kept woman to the reality of her position, our interest is continually diverted from the picture of the woman and her lover to the intricate portrayal of the furniture of the room (which a friend of Hunt's assures us was painted from an appropriate model). We see the rosewood of the piano, the hem of her dress, the glove on the floor, even the wallpaper in the farthest corner of the picture with equal distinctness. Or when we see Millais's *Ophelia,* we see each twig, leaf, and flower on the bank with a clarity so distinct that the brilliance of the picture's botanical scrupulousness threatens to overwhelm Ophelia herself. The effect of this unnatural clarity is to create the impression of a morbid intensity of vision. Robin Ironside describes this effect.

> It was, at first, as if the Brotherhood looked at the world without eyelids; for them, a livelier emerald twinkled in the grass, a purer sapphire melted into the sea. On the illuminated page that nature seemed to thrust before their dilated pupils, every floating, prismatic ray, each drifting filament of vegetation, was rendered, in all its complexity, with heraldic brilliance and distinctness; the floor of the forest was carpeted not merely with the general variegation of light and shadow, but was seen to be plumed with ferns receiving each in a particular fashion the shafts of light that fell upon them; there were not simply birds in the branches above, but the mellow ouzel was perceived fluting in the elm. . . . The Pre-Raphaelites transcribed nature analytically, "selecting nothing and rejecting nothing," and the labour that went into the copying of each particle was sharpened by a kind of frenzy which goaded them into a burnishing and polishing of their handiwork to a point beyond representation, at which it shone with a feverish clarity.[35]

The unnaturalness of vision created by the clarity of detail in their paintings is increased by their choice of subjects. Although they take truth to nature as their battle cry, they most often choose for their subjects not natural objects but aesthetic images. Ophelia, the scapegoat, Claudio and Isabella, the Lady of Shalott, Christ in the house of his parents, Lorenzo and Isabella, the hireling shepherd, Ferdinand and Ariel—all are literary images or religious symbols. The viewer feels a tension between the symbolic nature of the subject, which produces certain expectations of representation, and the naturalism of its portrayal. Even when the Pre-Raphaelites choose scenes from modern life for their paintings, they pose characters in such stylized attitudes of extreme emotion, like the woman in *The Awakened Conscience,* that the ultimate effect is quite unrealistic.

Struck by such obvious contradictions in their work, most critics have stressed the inconsistency of the Pre-Raphaelite aesthetic. Realistic techniques, carried to such an extreme that they cease to create a realistic effect, combined with unrealistic subjects have made most critics conclude that the poor men were dreadfully confused, perhaps even stupid, and that their art suffers from a fatal lack of focus.[36] Part of the problem is the inability of critics to understand Pre-Raphaelitism in the Pre-Raphaelites' own terms. Despite all their talk about aesthetics, the Pre-Raphaelites were not very good theorists. Most of the time what they were doing was different from what they said they were doing. The important task for critics is not to show the inconsistency of their aesthetic but to concentrate on why the Pre-Raphaelites never seemed to feel any inconsistency in their works, and to discover what kind of art this strange combination of seemingly contradictory impulses produces. As a recent writer on Holman Hunt said, "The important question is, by what means did the Pre-Raphaelites, not only with equanimity but with a sense of mission, combine attention to detail with religious symbolism, fidelity to inner experience with social realism, an historical approach to the Bible with Evangelical Faith." [37]

Of course part of the answer lies in certain scientific assumptions about reality some artists acquired during the nineteenth century. In his book on Victorian poetic theory, Alba Warren demonstrates that most Victorians held the conviction that truth was the end of art and that the amount of truth in a work of art measured its quality. Ruskin, of course, is the critic most zealous in his belief that great art is that art which contains the largest amount of truth. As part of his demand for truth he insisted on scientific accuracy in the representation of detail. His long chapters in *Modern Painters* on the truth of skies, of earth, of water, of mountains, and of plants are designed to aid painters in their pursuit of accurate natural detail. Ruskin was far too sensitive an artist and critic, however, to let his definition of truth get in the way of what he felt was good art. He always qualifies his demand for truth by asking for only as great an amount as would be consistent with beauty or harmony. The mental gymnastics he performs in proving that Turner was the first of the Pre-Raphaelites show how flexible Ruskin could make his definition of truth to nature. Other artists failed to adjust their beliefs to their judgment with his agility. Certainly part of the Pre-Raphaelite demand for absolute accuracy in the representation of minute detail resulted from a pseudoscientific insistence upon the quantity of truth in art. In reaction to the discredit science had cast on other forms of truth, they tried to represent religious symbols through the medium of "scientific truth," which they defined as accuracy in the representation of natural detail. Holman Hunt, for example, the primary Pre-Raphaelite theorist, felt each age was given its quota of knowledge and wisdom to contribute toward the final truth. The nineteenth-century quota was truth of the accurate representation of natural fact. If artists made use of that truth in their paintings, they would increase the total sum of truth the paintings communicated. Hunt's sense of mission about representing religious symbols with minute scientific realism springs from his conviction that the kind of truth most meaningful to the nineteenth century is scientific truth, and that religious symbols portrayed with scientific accuracy will thus acquire a new cogency.[88]

If the Pre-Raphaelites confusedly applied scientific criteria of truth to other areas of experience, they also turned detail to uses completely independent of science. Their use of nature in many ways resembles Tennyson's. The sensibility of the age led both Tennyson and the Pre-Raphaelites to an extraordinary interest in the minutiae of nature. Tennyson's charts of isobars spring from the same impulse as Hunt's sitting long hours after midnight, his feet wrapped in rags for extra warmth, to copy weeds in moonlight for *The Light of the World*, but the overly acute consciousness of detail in Tennyson's poetry and in Pre-Raphaelite painting was more than a blunder of their enthusiastic fervor for scientific accuracy. Like Tennyson, the Pre-Raphaelites managed to turn natural detail to purely expressionistic uses essentially independent of nature.

In their paintings with religious or literary symbols as subjects, the Pre-Raphaelites create a startling effect by the minute realism of their portrayal. The vulgarization of representational skills in the twentieth century makes it hard for us to realize how revolutionary the impact of these paintings was. The prosaicness of Millais's *Christ in the House of His Parents* shocked the major art critics and even Charles Dickens into passionate indignation. *Blackwood's* review announced that "such a collection of splay feet, puffed joints, and misshapen limbs was assuredly never before made within so small a compass." [39] Within a week after the picture was displayed, *Punch* printed a note, apparently by a doctor, who diagnosed the sacred figures of the painting as displaying every symptom of "scrufulous or strumous diathesis," [40] and Dickens called the carpenters men such as "might be undressed in any hospital where dirty drunkards, in a high state of varicose veins, are received." [41] By their insistent realism, the Pre-Raphaelites overturned the conventional iconography of the day. They created a tension in their pictures between the symbolic nature of the subject and the realism of its portrayal. Marianne Moore has said that poets should present "imaginary gardens with real toads in them," and the Pre-Raphaelites do precisely this. Furthermore, they make the warts on the toads so clear the garden no longer seems imaginary. Religious symbols are portrayed so realistically they become almost irreligious because, like Rossetti's blessed damozel, they insist so strongly on the fact of their physicality. By this exaggeratedly realistic portrayal of symbols, the paintings startle the viewer into rethinking those symbols' concrete meaning. Ruskin seems to understand this aspect of Pre-Raphaelitism when he asserts the value of representing symbolic events in their material veracity. The artist will either compel the spectator to believe the event really happened or make him detect his own incredulity and recognize that he had never asked himself if the event indeed was so.[42]

By their realistic portrayal of symbols, the Pre-Raphaelites were trying to create a viable symbolic art for the nineteenth century. Nineteenth-century artists had difficulty seeing the details of daily life as carrying a spiritual and human significance comparable to the significance they had carried in older cultures such as that of the Middle Ages. When artists attempted to make these details carry a sacramental value a sentimentalism resulted, in which events were laden with an emotional and spiritual significance far too heavy for them, as in Coventry Patmore's domestic epic, for example, *The Angel in the House*. In *Art and Visual Perception*, Rudolf Arnheim argues that a union between basic beliefs and the daily activities of living is necessary for a rich art and culture.

> the main virtue of any genuine culture would seem to be the capacity to experience the practical activities of living as tangible manifestations of basic principles. As long as getting a drink of water is felt—consciously or unconsciously—as obtaining sustenance from nature or God, as long as man's privilege and fate are symbolized for him in his labor, culture is safe. But when existence is limited to its specific material values, it ceases to be a symbol and thus loses the transparency on which all art depends. The very essence of art is the unity of idea and material realization.[43]

The deadness of conventional symbols and the inability to see the details of modern life as having symbolic resonance led to both Pre-Raphaelite medievalism and the Pre-Raphaelite attempt to portray these conventional symbols with scientific naturalism.[44] "The Blessed Damozel" and *The Scapegoat* are different paths to the same goal. Both try to restore a harmony between idea and visible fact that their artists were convinced modern life had lost, and by their use of detail both try to restore emotive power and physical presence to the symbol.

In an article on *The Scapegoat*, Herbert Sussman asserts that the central principle of Hunt's art, as well as that of the other naturalistic Pre-Raphaelites, was the fusion of representational accuracy and religious meaning in what may be called the naturalistic symbol. Sussman argues that this principle rests upon the transcendental assumption that material facts carry spiritual meanings. The Pre-Raphaelites pursue accurate representation so zealously because they believe as a result of this assumption that the more physically accurate a painting, the more spiritually meaningful it will be. According to Ruskin, the better the hoof and hair painting in a portrait of a goat, the more powerful it will be as a symbol.[45]

Ruskin, no doubt, did believe in the concept of the naturalistic symbol, and interpreted Pre-Raphaelite art accordingly. His assertion that painting should be particular, however, springs from very different impulses than does the Pre-Raphaelites' insistence upon particularity. Ruskin never argued that artists should pursue the accurate representation of detail to the neglect of other considerations; he said only that accurate representation of particulars created more truthful and consequently greater art. He saw preoccupation with detail as morbid: the German and Flemish painters, for example, had "a morbid habit of mind" that caused them "to lose sight of the balance and relations of things, so as to become intense in trifles, gloomily minute." [46] His view of extreme consciousness of detail suggests Tennyson's understanding of it rather than the Pre-Raphaelites'; he saw the

Pre-Raphaelite passion for representing minute detail as a
rather laudable excess in their scientific passion for truth. He
felt they were occasionally negligent and fell into a "morbid
indulgence of their own impressions," [47] but he never saw
this morbid intensity of vision as essential to their art.

Ruskin and Sussman completely misunderstand the Pre-
Raphaelite use of detail. No doubt Hunt and the other Pre-
Raphaelites were looking for naturalistic symbols. Hunt goes
to great pains to assert that the details in *The Light of the
World* were not derived from ecclesiastical or archaic symbolism but from "obvious reflectiveness." [48] Yet what is interesting about Pre-Raphaelite paintings is the way the minute
realism of representation interacts with the "naturalistic symbols." The superabundance and unnatural clarity of detail
together with the frequent artificiality of the attitude of the
subject, far from pushing the painting further toward natural
representation, push it back toward the realm of art. Both
the amount of detail and the posing of the subjects have a
stilling effect that makes the painting seem more like an
emblem than a natural object. The full presentation of each
element of the scene, like the simultaneous presentation of all
elements of a scene in the landscapes of medieval art, emphasizes the symbolic aspect of the objects. We do not see a
Pre-Raphaelite painting as a single impression of a scene as
it looks from one point of view at one moment. Rather, the
fullness of the presentation of each detail makes it fall apart
into pieces that can be individually explicated. Most critics
see this as a fault and conclude that the Pre-Raphaelites had
a very naive notion of realism, but it is an essential element
of the kind of art that they were trying to create. The detailed representation of even the smallest objects in each painting makes each one a possible focus of contemplation. The
paintings thus imply a symbolic view of the world, in which
each object can become instinct with meaning. By thus sin-
gling out each object, the Pre-Raphaelites build into their
painting stylistically the impetus to a sacramental view of
reality. At the same time the naturalism of the portrayal
pushes what had been a symbol toward status as a natural

object, the sheer quantity of detail pulls it back toward status as a symbol. Images are thus poised precariously and deliberately on the brink between being aesthetic objects and being natural objects. Such portrayal reflects an assumption about the way man perceives. Faced with a world of natural objects instinct with symbolic meaning, man can understand that meaning, by intensity of contemplation. The conscious elaboration of detail in Pre-Raphaelite art reveals just such a consciously symbol-making effort. Far from producing a fatal lack of integrity of focus, the combination of allegorical and highly realistic details suggests the process of symbolic perception.

The superabundance of detail also has an emotional effect. Its excessive clarity and brilliance echoes the intensity in the emotional attitude of most of the subjects and thus intensifies the emotional response of the viewer. In *The Scapegoat,* the sharply detailed representation of the salt, the goat's footprints, the broken twigs, and the bones of old goats suggests a morbid clarity of vision which increases the pathos of the image of the scapegoat. In *Ophelia,* the brilliance of the landscape almost absorbs Ophelia. She seems to be literally dying into the life of nature, and its vitality increases the poignancy of her human death.

This emotive use of detail is even more pronounced in Pre-Raphaelite pictures based on scenes taken from modern life. *The Awakened Conscience; The Long Engagement,* Arthur Hughes's painting of two lovers looking up at the sky with an expression of maudlin but genteel mournfulness; William Henry Windus's *Too Late,* a picture of a young swain returning to his village sweetheart to find her dying of consumption; Ford Madox Brown's *The Last of England,* a picture of two departing Australian emigrants—these pictures strike us as quintessentially Victorian. And what is so peculiarly Victorian about them is the combination of an intense emotion compressed into a small but melodramatic gesture, such as raising the eyes or clasping the hands, with a crowded, busy surface. They bring together the sentimentality of the era with the undigested detail of its decor and its architecture.

In these pictures, the Pre-Raphaelites were trying to represent inner states of strong feeling, to portray invisible areas of human emotion, and they found the resources of human gesture and expression very inadequate. This inadequacy explains the frequency of grotesque expressions and rigidly stylized attitudes in these pictures. The ghastly joy that possesses the face of the woman in *The Awakened Conscience* was the best Hunt could do to show what a moral transformation felt like. Because of the inadequacy of bodily posture and facial expression to convey states of extreme emotion, the Pre-Raphaelites turned to the use of landscape to convey the emotional intensity of their subjects. Ford Madox Brown describes exactly this strategy in talking about *The Last of England:* "The minuteness of detail which would be visible under such conditions of broad daylight I have thought necessary to imitate as bringing the pathos of the subject home to the beholder." [49] In other words, Brown depicts objects in the painting with unnatural distinctness in order to suggest the poignant clarity they have to a mind at a crisis such as leaving home forever. The clarity of detail thus helps express the peculiar emotional stress of the emigrants' situation to the beholder. Ruskin makes a similar analysis of the use of detail in Holman Hunt's *The Awakened Conscience.*

> . . . the careful rendering of the inferior details in this picture . . . is based on a truer principle of the pathetic than any of the common artistical expedients of the schools. Nothing is more notable than the way in which even the most trivial objects force themselves upon the attention of a mind which has been fevered by violent or distressful excitement. They thrust themselves forward with a ghastly and unendurable distinctness, as if they would compel the sufferer to count, or measure, or learn them by heart.[50]

Though we may be amused that, as one critic put it, "the inner movement of soul is so richly and factually a social vision of upholstery and interior decor," nevertheless, the particularity with which Hunt portrays the interior of the room conveys the emotional intensity of the moment as it heightens the woman's sensitivity to the objects that surround her. The distinctness of such banal tokens of her life as the rosewood furniture, the discarded glove, the freshly bound books suggests the terrible clarity of her awareness of what her life really is.

The use of detail in these pictures resembles the poetic use of detail to portray a morbid state of emotion in *Maud* or "The Bride's Prelude" or "My Sister's Sleep." Significantly, James Smetham, a minor Pre-Raphaelite painter, wrote that the stanzas about the shell in *Maud* "[answer] well to an unvarying condition of a mind in anguish, viz., to be riveted and fascinated by very little things." [51] The Pre-Raphaelite use of detail springs from a similar psychological insight. This use of detail in painting, however, depends upon the main figure of the painting functioning as a narrator would in a poem. We must see the landscape through his eyes, as a reflection of his emotion, much as we seem to see the house in Mariana through her eyes. But because this kind of projection is very difficult to attain in painting, the Pre-Raphaelite painters fail to manipulate detail to this effect as successfully as do the poets.

Humphrey House once defined the peculiar quality of the Victorian sensibility as a combination of hysteria and extreme literalness,[52] a combination that perfectly defines Pre-Raphaelite art. The Pre-Raphaelites were seeking expressionistic art to portray strong states of emotion, and by an accident of history they wound up seeking it through naturalism. As a result, they created a realism so exaggerated it became expressionistic. They use detail, much like Rossetti, to attain a subjective intensity in art and to give symbols a concrete sensuous immediacy, but Rossetti's poetry is ultimately more successful than Pre-Raphaelite painting in the ways it uses detail and more radical in the significance it attaches to it. Despite their emphasis on the physical reality of religious symbols, the Pre-Raphaelites want to maintain and even strengthen the symbolic dimension. They do not share Rossetti's insistence on

the independent value of the sensuous immediacy of the image, but rather use that immediacy to make the symbol convincing and thus meaningful to the viewer. Furthermore,
Rossetti's subjective selectivity in his use of detail is psychologically more profound and aesthetically more capable of
development. The Pre-Raphaelites went to nature, as did
Tennyson, to communicate states of hysterical and morbid
emotion essentially independent of it, but in doing so tried
to make nature communicate things difficult for it to convey.
Despite this aesthetic failure, their connection of aggressive
particularity with extreme, often morbid emotion bears a
fascinating similarity to this connection in the poetry of Tennyson and Rossetti. But to the Pre-Raphaelites this intense
consciousness of particulars did not suggest, as it did to Tennyson, loss of balance and relation in a world whose center
could not hold. Rather, in their painting, as well as in the
poetry of Rossetti, it gradually came to reflect the discovery
of a new center in the subjective perception of each individual.

2

"The World's Multitudinousness": Atomism and the Grotesque

The emerging sensitivity to particularity in the Victorian period demanded new ways of understanding both the world and the self. Because the Victorians could no longer depend upon the idea of type to organize particulars, they had to reform their sense of the world's structure. Were there principles of order and unity? What were they? What adjustments of understanding did they make necessary? The Victorians also had to reexamine their understanding of individual perception. Given the world's multiplicity and the particularity of individual consciousness, what kinds of knowledge were possible? Could man transcend the particularity of the world and his own experience in a perception that extended beyond the sensation of mere particulars? I will devote the next two chapters to discussing the ways in which writers resolved these problems, centering my discussions upon Browning and Hopkins, whose poetry undertakes to deal with both problems directly and fully.

In a criticism of Browning's poetry, Arnold wrote that poets "must begin with an Idea of the world in order not to be prevailed over by the world's multitudinousness." [1] Arnold felt the idea of the universal had to prevail over the particular in order to maintain the cultural and moral values to which he so desperately clung. To admit the primacy of the particular over the universal seemed to admit an epistemological and ethical relativism Arnold wanted to avoid. But the poetry of the Victorian period came to reverse Arnold's priorities. The characters in Browning's dramatic monologues and Hopkins's sense of inscape both spring from an insistence upon the priority of the individual over classification and a delight in the very multiplicity Arnold had condemned. Browning and Hopkins, different as they are in so many respects, have a similar understanding of the world's particularity. Both see the world composed of emphatically individual units, each propelled by its own peculiar energy. We have seen in the past chapter how Tennyson's and Rossetti's use of detail implied a sensitivity to particularity that threatened many of the assumptions the Victorians held about the universe. Browning and Hopkins, however, see the particular as the basis of a new order, a world united in the very multiplicity of its individual energies.

We can see Browning's emphasis on the distinctive energy of the individual in his portrayal of the natural world. Here, for example, is a description of a little girl eating and drinking from "The Englishman in Italy":

> Meantime, see the grape bunch they've brought you:
> The rain-water slips
> O'er the heavy blue bloom on each globe
> Which the wasp to your lips
> Still follows with fretful persistence:
> Nay, taste, while awake,
> This half of a curd-white smooth cheese-ball
> That peels, flake by flake,
> Like an onion, each smoother and whiter;
> Next, sip this weak wine
> From the thin green glass flask, with its stopper,
> A leaf of the vine;
> And end with the prickly-pear's red flesh
> That leaves through its juice
> The stony black seeds on your pearl-teeth.[2]

Browning presents each object in this passage with an intensity and emphasis that exceeds normal consciousness. He attains this effect by dwelling upon the differences between objects that give them individual characters. In writing about Browning's representation of color and form, C. H. Herford observes that Browning loves colors that bring out intensity and conflict and forms that have clear-cut outlines and sharply defined articulations.[3] Herford's observation perfectly describes Browning's portrayal of nature here. Browning emphasizes everything that contributes to visual and tactile impressions of distinctness. He dwells upon the bright colors of objects that separate them from their surroundings like the blue of the grapes or the white of the cheese, peculiar textures like the prickliness of the pear, and sharp lines dividing objects—the stony seeds against the girl's white teeth. Through this emphasis, Browning creates a sense of the individual energy of each object that defines its identity. Even static characteristics like texture and color seem active assertions.

By the distinctness of his definition of individual elements, Browning transforms objects or actions that appear to be units into aggregations of particulars. In "Sibrandus Schafnaburgensis," for example, Browning describes a book he had dropped into a hole in an old tree trunk a month before in revenge for its pedantic dullness.

> Here you have it, dry in the sun,
>   With all the binding all of a blister,
> And great blue spots where the ink has run,
>   And reddish streaks that wink and glister
> O'er the page so beautifully yellow:
>   Oh, well have the droppings played their tricks!
> Did he guess how the toadstools grow, this fellow?
>   Here's one stuck in his chapter six!
>
> How did he like it when the live creatures
>   Tickled and toused and browsed him all over,
> And worm, slug, eft, with serious features,
>   Came in, each one, for his right of trover?
> — When the water-beetle with great blind deaf face
>   Made of her eggs the stately deposit,

> And the newt borrowed just so much of the preface
>   As tiled in the top of his black wife's closet?

Browning changes a lifeless, static object into a location of a
crawling, vital conflux of life. Propelled by its peculiar energy,
each creature tries to transform the book into its own environment. In the process, they change it from a closed, completed
unit to a continually evolving stage on which natural elements
act out their individual identities. Even the colors the book
has turned help overcome our sense of it as a single object.
Their aggressiveness makes the book seem to be on the point
of disintegrating into an aggregate of disjunct elements—
blistered binding, blue spots, red streaks.

The emphasis in Browning's poetry on the distinctive energy propelling each object creates a sense of the world's fullness and multiplicity. The objects of his universe constantly
jostle one another. Each form of energy pushes against those
surrounding it in a fight for its own place, as in this landscape from "The Englishman in Italy":

> Place was grudged to the silver-grey fume-weed
>   That clung to the path,
> And dark rosemary ever a-dying
>   That, 'spite the wind's wrath,
> So loves the salt rock's face to seaward,
>   And lentisks as staunch
> To the stone where they root and bear berries,
>   And . . . what shows a branch
> Coral-colored, transparent, with circlets
>   Of pale seagreen leaves.

In its vision of the universe as an aggregation of particulars
in constant interaction, Browning's poetry resembles Darwinian biology and the atomism Lucretius describes in *De Rerum
Natura*. Both Lucretius and Darwin see the large units of the
natural world created and propelled by the energy of a mass
of particulars. For Lucretius, each seemingly unitary object
is a temporary aggregation of a countless number of individ-

ual atoms in perpetual motion and collision, and for Darwin,
type and species are artificial abstractions imposed upon a
constantly evolving "tangled bank" of individual life forms
involved in a struggle with each other for existence. Browning,
by focusing on the minute, the primitive, the bizarre particular, makes this vision emphatic. And this focus creates
what critics have often called the grotesque quality of Browning's poetry.

Grotesque was originally an art term describing a kind of
painting or sculpture that combined portions of human and
animal forms with foliage and flowers, often creating mon-
sters, half man and half beast, but the word soon came to
describe anything characterized by distortion, exaggeration, in-
congruity, deformity, extravagance. The term has frequently
been used in literary criticism, but in connection with so
many very different writers—Browning, Kafka, Rabelais, Dickens, Chaucer, and Dostoevesky, to name just a few—that precise definition is difficult. On its simplest, most colloquial
level, the grotesque is the unusual that violates our tolerance
for the unusual; it is the aggressively incongruous or bizarre.
When this extreme insistence on the incongruous becomes an
ordering principle in literature, we call that literature grotesque. Writers attain the grotesque in very different ways
and for very different ends, but the grotesque always seems to
express the source of disorder in the writer's world. For the
Middle Ages, the grotesque is associated with evil, particularly
appetitive evil, which transforms man into beast. For modern
writers, the grotesque most often expresses not the evil of the
self but the absurdity of a world man can no longer understand or control. Like the meaning, the technique of the
grotesque is one of disorder, of purposeful confusion of categories. Medieval gargoyles are strange combinations of man
and beast; in Kafka, a man wakes up to find himself a cock-
roach. This mixture of categories dissolves the borders between the human world, the animal world, and in the twentieth century, even the mechanical world. Animals and objects
often take on a human character, becoming unpredictable and

terrifyingly independent, while the human becomes bestial, mechanistic.

The first to link Browning's poetry with the label *grotesque* was Walter Bagehot. In a review of *Enoch Arden and Other Poems* and *Dramatis Personnae,* Bagehot differentiates three kinds of English poetry: the pure, the ornate, and the grotesque.[4] *Pure* poetry describes the type, or the concrete universal, with the greatest simplicity possible, representing its subject with only the number of strokes necessary to delineate it fully. It embodies the ideal of classical art, and Bagehot sees its finest English examples in Wordsworth and Milton. The *ornate,* on the other hand, portrays the type with as much elaboration as it will bear. If the pure suggests the classical, the ornate suggests the baroque. Bagehot's justification for the ornate is a peculiar one: it is most appropriate, he feels, for the "unpleasing type." It makes "people who sell fish about the country" (which Bagehot insists is all that Enoch Arden did), a pleasant object for an aristocratic and fastidious reading public to contemplate. The grotesque, however, has an entirely different focus from either the pure or the ornate. Both of these aim at the representation of type, of a concrete object or circumstance—whether the sunrise on Westminster Bridge or a dirty sailor who did not go home to his wife—that suggests the universal. The grotesque does just the contrary.

> It takes the type, so to say, *in difficulties.* It gives a representation of it in its minimum development, amid the circumstances least favourable to it, just while it is struggling with obstacles, just where it is encumbered with incongruities. It deals, to use the language of science, not with normal types but with abnormal specimens; to use the language of old philosophy, not with what nature is striving to be, but with what by some lapse she has happened to become.[5]

Bagehot's discussion of the grotesque is encumbered by his standard of the type; nevertheless, he identifies one of its most essential characteristics, its concern with "abnormal specimens."

Because of this attention to the abnormal, this dissolution of categories the grotesque creates a sense of a world gone out of control, an unreliable world in which we can no longer orient ourselves.[6] This lack of control can be either amusing, as in Rabelais, or terrifying, as in Kafka or Dostoevsky. Whether the grotesque is funny or frightening probably depends on a writer's sense of order. Because of its doubt of the ultimate existence of order, the twentieth century has reacted to the grotesque largely with horror. In Browning, on the other hand, the grotesque is a source of exuberance and vitality. The principle of the grotesque in Browning derives from the individuality of the forms of life's energy, and Browning attains the grotesque by his bizarre location of this energy. As G. K. Chesterton observes, nature might mean grass to Walt Whitman and flowers to William Wordsworth, but it means funguses and ocean polyps to Robert Browning.[7] When we think of Browning's natural world, we think of newts, shrimp, mushrooms, jellyfish, and water beetles; when we think of his human world, we think of Caliban, Mr. Sludge, Porphyria's lover. By this strange location of life's energy, Browning makes us comprehend life in its particularity rather than its typicality. He breaks down our usual sympathies and destroys our expectations of significant focus to give us a vision of a world of emphatically peculiar energies, each continually in motion.

In the eccentricity of his characters and the peculiar languages he creates for them Browning resembles Dickens. Both see a world composed of peculiar, self-contained bodies, each soliloquizing its way through life. But the grotesque is ultimately more terrifying in Dickens because his characters are finally helpless to control either themselves or the social mechanism that contains them. Browning's characters are frightening only in the success with which they do control their environments. Browning is fascinated with the power of the will to create and control its world, and some of his

characters—the Duke of "My Last Duchess," Porphyria's
lover, Bishop Blougram—seem almost successful. Yet even
in these poems there is a suggestion of a stage trick about
them, as if Browning is ready to pop out from behind his
mask at any moment, which makes the grotesque an amusing
game rather than a terrifying possibility. Despite the difference
between the ultimate effects of the two writers, however, they
are similar in the necessity both feel to include such a range
of eccentricity in their fictional worlds. The reason lies, I
think, in the breakdown of the idea of type. In older litera-
tures the author could speak for everyman through an ideal
type, were it Adam or Tom Jones; but as the sense of norm
disintegrates, everyman becomes as various and peculiar as
the number of individuals the world contains. In the face of
the world's irreducible particularity, the writer can either re-
strict the authority of his work to a statement about or
through a single eccentric consciousness, as does Conrad or
Proust, for example. Or he can suggest in his fictional world
such a range of existential possibilities that his works attain a
sense of universality not from idealization or typicality but
from sheer inclusiveness.

Paradoxically, the inclusiveness and particularly of Browning's world results in a new basis for organic unity. In dis-
pelling our usual assumptions about the location of life, by
creating a sense of energy in unexpected places, he makes
everything in his world, from the most primitive jellyfish to
man himself, appear to exist on the same plane of vital particularity.

"The Englishman in Italy," for example, euphorically celebrates the vitalistic harmony of nature by animating each
element of the landscape. Browning matches the intense definition of the minute that we have already observed with animation of the huge, mountains and islands, to make the hills
dance with precisely the same kind of energy as the wasp. By
propelling everything in his poetic world with the same vital
force, Browning dissolves the separation of man and the physical universe, in the way that so often marks the grotesque.

The children scampering around the fisherman seem no different from the shrimp in his basket.

> No seeing our skiff
> Arrive about noon from Amalfi,
> —Our fisher arrive,
> And pitch down his basket before us,
> All trembling alive
> With pink and grey jellies, your sea fruit;
> You touch the strange lumps,
> And months gape there, eyes open, all manner
> Of horns and of humps,
> Which only the fisher looks grave at,
> While round him like imps
> Cling screaming the children as naked
> And brown as his shrimps.

Perhaps "Caliban Upon Setebos" contains the most extraordinary identification of the human, or semihuman, with the natural world. Caliban seems to be an animal, propelled by his peculiar life force, just like the creatures he describes.

> ('Will sprawl, now that the heat of day is best,
> Flat on his belly in the pit's much mire,
> With elbows wide, fists clenched to prop his chin.
> And, while he kicks both feet in the cool slush,
> And feels about his spine small eft-things course,
> Run in and out each arm, and make him laugh:
> And while above his head a pompion-plant,
> Coating the cave-top as a brow its eye,
> Creeps down to touch and tickle hair and beard,
> And now a flower drops with a bee inside,
> And now a fruit to snap at, catch and crunch,—
> He looks out o'er yon sea which sunbeams cross
> And recross till they weave a spider-web,
> (Meshes of fire, some great fish breaks at times,)
> And talks to his own self, howe'er he please,
> Touching that other, whom his dam called God.

The pompion plant creeping down the front of the cave to
tickle Caliban's eye and beard, the sunbeams crossing and re-
crossing to weave a fiery web, and Caliban sprawling and kick-
ing in the mud and speculating on his God all seem alike
individual creatures acting out their autonomous identities.

In the last chapter we spoke of particularity only in relation
to consciousness and to impressions: objects have appeared
particular through the perspective of individual awarenesses.
The sense of particularity I am describing in Browning, however, goes beyond individually distinctive perceptions to the
identities of objects themselves, and this extension of the
concept of particularity to the processes of nature represents
a great change in its significance. We have seen how sensitivity to particularity first threatened the Victorians with the
loss of those generalizations which fixed man's relationship to
his universe. Because individual impressions seemed to have
no significance beyond themselves, man's relationship to any
object in nature became an arbitrary one of seemingly disproportionate focus, and the connection between man and his
world threatened to reduce itself to particular visual sensation. In Browning, however, particularity becomes the principle that reunites man with his world. All things are related
through the vital force of their own identities propelling
them. The energy of the particular creates an identification
between man and matter that reconnects man to his universe
in a way the very sensibility to particularity had threatened to
destroy.

The way Browning reached his vision of particularity reveals
much about the ways particularity threatened the Victorians'
sense of identity: he came to this vision through a search for
the absolute. The heroes of his early poems, *Pauline* and
Paracelsus, aspire to know the absolute truth, but their desire to know is torn between two contradictory impulses, one
toward an identification with the Absolute Mind or with God
and the other toward a Protean consciousness "which would
be all, have, see, know, taste, feel, all," even life's minutest
forms. Although a Protean consciousness suggests a search for

particular knowledge, as opposed to the quest for general truth implied by the desire for the absolute, Browning's heroes attack the two quests in equally absolutist frames of mind. The hero of *Pauline* must know either the Absolute face to face or *all* of life's particulars. Behind these styles of knowledge lie two related and equally absolutist myths of the self: the myth of the magnificently independent and wholly unfettered self and the opposite myth of the totally obliterated self,[8] or in Keats's terms, the "egotistical sublime" and "negative capability." The confusion of *Pauline* is in large part created by the hero's vacillation between these two forms of knowledge and of self-consciousness. The hero cannot reconcile his desire to abandon himself to the process of life with his magnificent feeling of the self's supreme importance. The Protean life process cannot absorb his boundless energy but neither can he discover the Absolute Mind he seeks. In *Paracelsus*, Browning externalizes the conflict of these two impulses toward the absolute in the figures of the poet Aprile, who would love infinitely and so vainly tries to apprehend all the forms of life's particularity, and the philosopher Paracelsus, who would know infinitely and dies still aspiring. We see the dialectic again in Browning's essay on Shelley, where he opposes the objective poet, who would reproduce all the phenomena of the external world, and the subjective poet, who tries to express the Ideas of Plato, things in their absolute truth, which he can most closely approach through examining his own soul.

The heroes' failure to attain the absolute in these early poems has important implications concerning Browning's own poetic development. The poems are largely autobiographical; in them, Browning confronts his romantic heritage and his inability to know the absolute face to face. Although he implies in *Paracelsus* and in the essay on Shelley that the ideal poet is a synthesis of the objective and the subjective poet, of Aprile and Paracelsus, his own adoption of the dramatic monologue form shortly after writing these poems seems to be an acceptance of the Protean response to the challenge of the absolute. J. Hillis Miller argues that the dramatic monologue is the strategy Browning adopts to confront God: he will enter all life's created forms, since he cannot confront Him face to face.[9] Miller emphasizes the quest for the absolute he sees still implicit in Browning's use of the dramatic monologue and the absolutist myths of the self that this quest implies. But a more profound significance of Browning's adoption of the dramatic monologue, lies in his embrace of an entirely different style of knowing, impossible for the early Victorians, and a modification of even those absolutist myths of the self that lie behind the Protean strain of Romantic Prometheanism.

One of the central and most cataclysmic experiences of Victorian literature and autobiography is the conversion experience. One thinks of *Sartor Resartus,* Mill's *Autobiography,* Newman's *Apologia.* The pain experienced by such writers when they feel old beliefs fail them and the psychological necessity they show for a dramatic conversion to another set of beliefs reflect a need for a stable and absolute source of identity. Although the frequency of conversions in the period betokens a collapse of traditional sources of stability, the traumatic form the experience often took shows that the need for absolute values as the foundation of identity still persisted. The dramatic monologue, however, shows a new ability to make rapid shifts of ideas, images, and ideology; the very form implies ease in changing identity; it suggests the possibility of a new and un-Romantic Protean style of life process, which emphasizes flux and change, not universality, and which Robert Jay Lifton has defined as the predominant pattern of identity in our day.[10] The form sees no ideal standard or model of identity, no one set of stable institutions or symbols that define a general type or ideal every man must emulate, but only a series of particular possibilities, each of which in part generates its own standards of judgment. Of course Browning never totally abandons an objective distance from which to judge his figures, but that judgment can only be made by actually experiencing the peculiar way each character defines himself. The dramatic monologue applies the principle of particularity we have seen in other areas of experience to the source of identity itself. Even the absolutist myth of the totally obliterated self implicit in the figure of Proteus and by analogy in the figure of the poet himself is greatly qualified by an insistence upon the process, the incompleteness, and the particularity of experience, even of the poet's exploration.

The novel can create a closeness to the inward moral being of an individual that suggests a sensitivity to the particularity of identity similar to that of the dramatic monologue. In *The Rise of the Novel*, Ian Watt argues that the novel is the literary form that expresses the realism and individualism characteristic of the modern attitude toward experience. The development of the Victorian novel can in part be seen as a movement toward even greater sensitivity to the particularity of experience than the eighteenth century novel suggests. We can see this in the eccentricity of Dickens's characters. George Eliot states her difference from Fielding precisely in terms of her interest in particulars rather than universals.

A Great historian, as he insisted on calling himself, who had the happiness to be dead a hundred and twenty years ago, and so to take his place among the colossi whose huge legs our living pettiness is observed to walk under, glories in his copious remarks and digressions as the least imitable part of his work, and especially in those initial chapters to the successive books of his history, where he seems to bring his arm chair to the proscenium and chat with us in all the lusty ease of his fine English. . . . We belated historians must not linger after his example . . . I at last have so much to do in unravelling certain human lots, and seeing how they were woven and interwoven, that all the light I can command must be concentrated on this particular web, and not dispersed over that tempting range of relevancies called the universe.[11]

Eliot's call for the reader's empathy for even her most un-
sympathetic characters—Bulstrode or Casaubon—suggests an
effort similar to Browning's to understand a range of possible
identities, some of which are morally or psychologically alien,
in their own terms. Like Browning, Eliot implies that to understand an individual we must experience his sense of the
world, and that to understand the universal we must experience a multitude of particulars.

Poetry, however, has traditionally been more primarily concerned with the universal than has the novel, and Browning's
achievement lies in his development of a poetry similar to the
novel in its concentration on particular experience. One of
the reasons the Victorian poets felt that the dramatic monologue was so congenial a form is no doubt the similarity of
the dramatic monologue to the novel not only in subject but
in its tendency to make particular rather than universal statements. Browning's contribution to the dramatic monologue is
the grotesqueness of his characters. Tennyson's, Arnold's and
Rossetti's characters suggest emotional states more often than
individual personalities. Browning's characters are emphatically individual.

Like his sense of nature, his sense of human personality is
dynamic. His poems apprehend people in the midst of the
activities that most reveal their individuality, and the meaning
of the poems lies largely just in the peculiar energy his characters display. This energy causes each character, much like
the animals inhabiting the book in "Sibrandus Schafnaburgensis," to construct his own peculiar environment from the
world around him. J. Hillis Miller observes how each living
creature in Browning's world creates around itself a sphere,
a bubble, an aura or milieu that is its habitation in the
world.[12] For Andrea del Sarto, "a common greyness silvers
everything;" for Fra Lippo Lippi, the world "means intensely
and means good." In each of his dramatic monologues, Browning presents not just a particular character, but a distinct
phenomenology, an entire particular world as that character
experiences it. Often he creates this world through a poetic

particularity, an unnaturally sharp representation of detail
which emphasizes that character's peculiar perspective. "Caliban Upon Setebos" contains the most extraordinary use of detail in this way. In the poem Browning uses the details of
which Caliban is conscious not just to form a world but to
generate an entire cosmogony. Caliban reasons by observing
or recalling some fact he has perceived about the natural
world and then using that to construct his concept of his
deity.

> He is strong and Lord.
> 'Am strong myself compared to yonder crabs
> That march now from the mountain to the sea;
> 'Let twenty pass, and stone the twenty-first,
> Loving not, hating not, just choosing so.
> 'Say the first straggler that boasts purple spots
> Shall join the file, one pincer twisted off;
> 'Say, this bruised fellow shall receive a worm,
> And two worms he whose nippers end in red;
> And it likes me each time, I do: so He.
> . . . .
> Meanwhile, the best way to escape His ire
> Is, not to seem too happy. 'Sees, himself,
> Yonder two flies, with purple films and pink,
> Bask on the pompion-bell above: kills both.
> 'Sees two black painful beetles roll their ball
> On head and tail as if to save their lives:
> Moves them the stick away they strive to clear.

Although Caliban's sensitivity to particularity is one of the
ways Browning suggests the theological myopia that is the
specific subject of this poem, it also reflects an inherent energy
thrusting itself out and forming a world in its own image in
a way analogous to that of any of Browning's characters. The
image of the blue vein on the Madonna's breast used by the
bishop in ordering his tomb at St. Praxed's church has a
particularity verging on the grotesque, similar to that of Caliban's images. The more bizarre, the more aggressively in-

congruous and particular the images, the more they increase
our consciousness of an absolutely individual energy acting
out its identity.

When critics speak of the grotesque in Browning, however,
they usually refer to the style rather than the content of his
verse.[13] The common element that readers see producing the
grotesque style in Browning is in "insistent, almost willful,
delight in inchoateness." [14] One critic has called Browning a
"semantic stutterer"; he has a great many things to say and
they all try to rush out simultaneously, producing sentences
all dashes and parentheses.[15] He refuses to disown or subordinate any of the directions in which his energy takes him. A
typical passage is this one from *Pippa Passes:*

> Meantime, what lights my sunbeam on,
> Where settles by degrees the radiant cripple?
> Oh, is it surely blown, my martagon?
> New-blown and ruddy as St. Agnes' nipple,
> Plump as the flesh-bunch on some Turk bird's poll!
> Be sure if corals, branching 'neath the ripple
> Of ocean, bud there,—fairies watch unroll
> Such turban flowers; I say, such lamps disperse
> Thick red flames through that dusk green universe!
> I am queen of thee floweret;
> And each fleshy blossom
> Preserve I not—(safer
> Than leaves that enbower it,
> Or shells that embosom)
> —From weevil and chafer?
> Laugh through my pane then; solicit the bee;
> Gibe him, be sure; and, in midst of thy glee,
> Love thy queen, worship me!

Pippa refuses to be satisfied with any one formulation of a
perception. When her attention is diverted from the sunbeam
to the martagon, she compares it to St. Agnes' nipple, a tur-
key's head, and coral, but none of these metaphors is sub-
ordinated to its object of comparison. Rather, each has its

own emphatic energy that carries it away from the central focus of the passage. Because of the extraordinary distinctness Browning gives to each metaphor, we become aware of them more as independent objects than as points of comparison. The coral even spawns a group of metaphors of its own— turban flowers, lamps, flame—to rival the martagon.

Browning's use of syntax increases the independent energy of his metaphors. Browning tends to make the elements of a perception parallel rather than subordinate to each other. In the passage above, each metaphor has either its own sentence or its own independent clause. Even within sentences, Browning weakens the syntactic connection between parts by inserting modifiers in awkward places and by separating those modifiers—by dashes, by parentheses, by the omission of connectives like "that" or "which," by their own length and elaboration—as far as possible from the sentence around them. For example, the phrase "safer than leaves that embower it, / Or shells that embosom" is separated by dashes and parentheses from its sentence. The use of the adjective "safer" for the adverb "more safely" and the elaboration "shells that embosom" after "leaves that embower" further leads the reader to perceive the entire adverbial clause as a separate unit. The effect of the syntactic disruption and elaboration of modifiers is to make the reader perceive passages of Browning's poetry not as single integrated ideas but as numerous disjunct impulses shooting out in all directions.

This independence of syntactic units is easy to see and to justify in Browning's conversational poems. Passages like the two following use expletives, repetitions, sentence fragments, and sudden leaps of thought to portray the dramatic situation and the immediate emotions and preoccupations of the speaker.

> Now, don't sir! Don't expose me! Just this once!
> This was the first and only time, I'll swear,—
> Look at me,—see, I kneel,—the only time,
> I swear I ever cheated,—yes, by the soul

> Of Her who hears—(your sainted mother, sir!)
> All, except this last accident, was truth—
> This little kind of slip!—and even this,
> It was your own wine, sir, the good champagne,
> (I took it for Catawba,—you're so kind)
> Which put the folly in my head!
>   ["Mr. Sludge, 'The Medium' "]
> Vanity, saith the preacher, vanity!
> Draw round my bed: is Anselm keeping back?
> Nephews—sons mine ... ah God, I know not! Well—
> She, men would have to be your mother once,
> Old Gandolf envied me, so fair she was!
> ["The Bishop Orders His Tomb at Saint Praxed's Church"]

In the first passage, Browning uses repeated exclamations and sentence fragments to dramatize the progression from Sludge's initial hysteria at being discovered through his attempts to use various ploys to manipulate his hearer—kneeling, calling upon his listener's mother, flattering his taste in wine, his kindness. As Sludge begins to regain his sense of self-possession, the ploys become more complex, more cunningly manipulative, and the syntax gets more involved. In the opening passage of "The Bishop Orders His Tomb," Browning stages the scene by combining a conventional trope on the vanity of interest in things of the world with the bishop's call for his "nephews" to gather round his bed. Then immediately Browning shows the bishop's main preoccupations in his admission to himself that the nephews are sons, in his characteristic response to that admission by an apostrophe of resigned doubt—"ah God, I know not"—and in his justification for the sin in the mother's beauty, made more important by Gandolf's envy. The broken syntax of the last sentence, with its interruption of the bishop's thought of his sons' mother by the thought of Gandolf, shows the principle importance the rivalry has in the bishop's mind.

We can thus see that Browning prefers paratactic to syntactic structures, for he wishes to emphasize emotional and dramatic connections rather than logical ones. This is apparent even in Browning's more philosophical monologues, which show a similar independence of syntactic elements. In the following passage, from *The Ring and the Book,* the Pope meditates on Pompilia's resistance to Guido's assault at the inn.

> But, brave,
> Thou at first prompting at what I call God,
> And fools call Nature, didst hear, comprehend,
> Accept the obligation laid on thee,
> Mother elect, to save the unborn child,
> As brute and bird do, reptile and the fly,
> Ay and, I nothing doubt, even tree, shrub, plant
> And flower o' the field, all in a common pact
> To worthily defend the trust of trusts,
> Life from the Ever Living: didst resist—
> Anticipate the office that is mine—
> And with his own sword stay the upraised arm,
> The endeavor of the wicked, and defend
> Him who—again in my default—was there
> For visible providence: one less true than thou
> To touch i' the past, less practised in the right,
> Approved so far in all docility
> To all instruction,—how had such an one
> Made scruple "Is this motion a decree?"
> It was authentic to the experienced ear
> O' the good and faithful servant.

[ll. 1071–1071]

The most striking stylistic element of this passage is the way the Pope restates each phrase in words with different theological implications—"what I call God / And fools call Nature," "that trust of trusts, / Life from the Ever Living," "didst resist— / anticipate the office that is mine." This repeated paraphrastic amplification of dependent phrases, although entirely grammatical, creates a sentence so unwieldy it is almost incoherent. But what Browning loses in syntactic coherence he gains in rhetorical effect. What the passage gives us is not a summary of the plot, which we know well enough at this point in the poem, but a sense of the complexity of the Pope's mind, of the care and subtlety with which he weighs and explores the spiritual implications of each judgment he makes. As in his more dramatic poems, Browning achieves psychological mimesis by choosing styles in which the logic created by syntactic coherence is unimportant, or insignificant. And by avoiding the normally expected syntax, Browning succeeds in making the elements of the sentence each appear as an independent psychic impulse.

Browning's style in this way suggests a sense of particularity similar to the one we have seen in his depiction of nature and character. The syntactical incoherence critics have called the grotesque in Browning's poetry results from an indulgent regard for the individual energy of each element of a perception without regard for the structure of the whole. This sense of individual energies is suggested even by Browning's words themselves. He chooses unpronounceable clusters of consonants —Sibrandus Schafnaburgensis, Schramm, Bluphocks, Sludge —calling attention to each individual sound. Each letter, like each element of perception, jostles the others, fighting for its place and identity. The clusters of letters create a fullness of sound, like the fullness of his landscapes or his sentences, where many opposing things try to exist at once.

Browning disrupts the normal patterns of language to make them reflect the unique form of each perception, but behind his effort lies a skepticism about the capacity of language to express the structure of our experience. In *The Ring and the Book,* the Pope meditates on man's use of language, in a way that reflects this skepticism.

> —Why, can he tell you what a rose is like,
> Or how the birds fly, and not slip to false
> Though truth serve better? Man must tell his mate
> Of you, me and himself, knowing he lies,
> Knowing his fellow knows the same,—will think
> "He lies, it is the method of a man!"

And yet will speak for answer "It is truth"
To him who shall rejoin "Again a lie!"
Therefore this filthy rags of speech, this coil
Of statement, comment, query and response,
Tatters all too contaminate for use,
Have no renewing . . .

[ll. 364–75]

The syntactical confusion, the sudden leaps of thought in Browning's poetry expose his conviction, as one critic put it, of "the fluid, messy, almost runny, nature of experience which continually evades the hard and resistant formulations of language." [16] Ultimately, only by violating its syntactical logic can language be made to represent the unordered multiplicity of elements in our experience.

From Browning's use of language and his use of the dramatic monologue emerges a pluralistic universe, in which contrary forces that no single point of view can totally incorporate exist side by side. This view, implicit in the form of the dramatic monologue, is made explicit in the structure of a number of longer poems. *The Ring and the Book,* as E. D. H. Johnson has shown in a study relating the poem to William James's concept of a pluralistic universe, suggests such a view by its structure of twelve books, each supplying a different perspective upon the poem's events.[17] Although some perspectives reveal more than others, no one perspective reveals the whole truth. The red, the green, and the blue of partial perspectives must combine to produce the white light of truth.[18] In Browning's plays, as well, written before and during the main period of his writing of the dramatic monologues, the characters serve less to advance the dramatic action than to suggest the coexistence of different perspectives upon a situation. The confusion in *In A Balcony* results from its three characters interpreting the same events in utterly different ways, and the main function of the subordinate characters in *Paracelsus* and *Sordello* is to provide contrasting perspectives to the points of view of the main characters.

Another adaptation of dramatic form to suggest the plurality of the universe is *Pippa Passes*. The poem tells the story of a single day, the yearly holiday, in the life of Pippa, a little girl who winds silk at a mill in a small Italian town called Asolo. The poem consists of four sections, "Morning," "Noon," "Evening," and "Night," each of which presents a crisis, the scene of which Pippa happens to pass, in the lives of four of Asolo's citizens. Although the poem is written in dramatic dialogue, neither the character development nor the action is continuous through its four sections. Although Pippa passes by in each section, she is more a symbolic force than a character. The lack of narrative sequence between episodes creates the impression of several diverse actions playing themselves out in the same place on the same day. To increase this sense of diversity, Browning selects his characters and episodes to display as many extreme contrasts as possible. The characters represent all manner of person, from prostitute to bishop. They have occupations ranging from revolutionary assassin to artist. They embody all kinds of love—love of a woman, love of country, love of God—and all degrees of good and evil.

These contrasts among the characters and episodes imply the coexistence of many different realities. The figure of Pippa, however, provides a unity to all this multiplicity. At each moment of moral crisis in the poem, Pippa happens to sing a song in the hearing of the characters involved that inspires them to make the right decision. Her songs give a melodramatic similarity to the episodes Browning has so insistently contrasted. This similarity implies a common potential for moral awareness, courage, and faith among all the characters, whatever direction it may take. Their responsiveness to Pippa's song suggests a responsiveness to the spiritual potential of human life. Pippa's language, as we showed above, associates her with the energy of the particulars in the natural world. She abandons herself to the distinctive life of each object her eye lights upon—the sunbeam, the coral, the martagon. Pippa's association with both nature's vitality and man's potential for moral goodness identifies the two as parallel life forces. Man's moral energy is a natural energy akin to the force that drives a toadstool or a sunbeam into its distinctive shape, and combines with them to give a vitalistic harmony to the universe.

The simplicity of the resolutions Pippa inspires makes the poem difficult for the modern reader. In a world where God seems noticeably absent, little girls cannot go around singing "God's in his heaven, / All's right with the world" without creating a sense that the resolutions brought about in this way are poetically and morally unearned. Browning's poem contains a tension, similar to that in Dickens's novels, between the simplicity of its moral resolutions and the grotesqueness and complexity of its world. This moral simplicity shows that Browning's ultimate sense of the meaning of the universe is morally and religiously quite conventional. What is modern about Browning is his sense of the way men comprehend the truth. In portraying the moral knowledge that Pippa brings out in four highly contrasted episodes, Browning suggests that the meaning of this knowledge is particular, experiential, plural. He matches sensitivity to the multitudinousness of the natural world with sensitivity to the plurality of significations man attaches to it. Just as each being of the natural world defines its identity through its distinctive energy, so perceptions show their truth only in the experiences in which they occur.

Nowhere is the experiential nature of truth more clearly defined than in *The Ring and the Book*. The poem has an almost unbearable prolixity. Browning tells the story ten times from the perspectives of nine characters in addition to several times from his own perspective. Schooled in modern fictional techniques, the reader might easily assume this structure implies a relativist view of reality, but such is not the case. The poem contains emphatically absolute standards of value. It is clear from the very beginning that Pompilia is good and Guido is evil. This prolixity does demonstrate, however, that man can understand the truth of a judgment only when he understands the many particular circumstances, experiences, and perspectives from which it arises. Only in this sense is the poem relativistic.[19] The ten perspectives Browning provides show that judgment depends upon the peculiar values, perception, and character of the judge. Likewise, the events of the poem demonstrate that judgment must accommodate itself to the specific situation involved. All the judgments of the poem made according to general expectations or typical behavior are overturned. Although Pompilia and Caponsacchi may appear to be adulterers according to a conventional interpretation of their actions, their individual characters and predicaments reveal that they are not. Likewise, all the institutional judgments of the poem—the Governor's, the Archbishop's, the Court's— prove false or inadequate because they are formed on the basis of general laws that are dead to the peculiar exigencies of Pompilia's and Guido's situation. An individual moral judgment—the Pope's—which tries to ferret out the particular motivation or the "seed of act" of each character, is the most authentic moral judgment of the poem.

In the course of his monologue, the Pope imagines Euripides confronting him and challenging his understanding.

> Pope, dost thou dare pretend to punish me,
> For not descrying sunshine at midnight,
> Me who crept all-fours, found my way so far—
> While thou rewardest teachers of the truth,
> Who miss the plain way in the blaze of noon.
>
> [ll. 1780–84]

Euripides demands from the Pope an experiential understanding of the truth of his life. By the profuse detail of the poem, which forces the reader to confront seemingly irrelevant circumstances of all the speakers' lives, Browning stresses not the relativity of truth in a metaphysical sense but the existential nature of all value and belief. The structure of the poem demonstrates a conviction similar to that of the modern existentialists that the truth of religious and moral values is only seen and believed (and in this sense only exists) in the experiencing of them. Their truth is plural, particular, existential.

The dramatic monologue can provide such existential comprehension of the truth because it forces the reader to view

the world of the speaker from the inside. The grotesqueness of
the characters Browning creates emphatically calls attention to
this approach. Because the speakers have perspectives very different from that of the reader and because Browning himself is
usually ironic rather than tragic in his vision of them, rarely
allowing them to come to self-discovery or revelation, immediate identification with many of Browning's characters is difficult. Our first reaction to a Guido, a Johannes Agricola, a
Porphyria's lover, a Mr. Sludge, a Caliban is a sense of their
eccentricity that distances and differentiates them from us.
Nevertheless, the form of the dramatic monologue puts the
reader in the position of the speaker. While the characters'
grotesquesness accentuates their particularity, the form of the
poem demands we comprehend them through experiencing the
way they see the world.

Browning's existential apprehension of belief implies a historicism that emerges quite naturally from the intellectual climate of the age. Just as the Victorians saw in all the physical
sciences the development of a historical sense, they saw in the
social sciences the development of a conviction of historical
relativity. Their consciousness of the particularity and multiplicity of the natural world was matched by a consciousness of
those same characteristics of the historical world. The writings
of Ruskin, of Carlyle, of Arnold, and above all of Pater display
a sensitivity to the individual character, the peculiar temper of
each historical and artistic epoch.

This developing historicism had its roots more in the Victorians' feelings about their own age than in any discovery
about the past. Because of its experience of rapid and continuous change, the Victorian age was the first to become self-
conscious about its own modernity. Essays like Mill's *Spirit of
the Age* or Carlyle's "Characteristics" represent the beginning
of that historical self-consciousness that obsesses us today, which
seeks to define the present, at the very time it is being experienced, as a distinct historical epoch. Implicit in this self-
consciousness is a sense of the difference and distance of past
historical periods from one's own. The age produced a number

of literary works—Ruskin's *Stones of Venice* and *Modern Painters,* Carlyle's *Past and Present* and *The French Revolution,* even Pater's *The Renaissance*—that appear to be histories but in fact create historical myths. These myths seek to end the dislocation from which the age was suffering by defining its difficulties through its difference from the past.

Writers of this emerging literary historicism felt it especially important to imagine the existential reality—the quotidien world view—of past cultures, in their effort to gain perspective on their own. Browning's historical dramatic monologues—"Cleon," "An Epistle from Karshish," "Fra Lippo Lippi," "Andrea del Sarto," "The Bishop Orders His Tomb at Saint Praxed's Church" (of which Ruskin wrote no other modern work told as much of the Renaissance spirit, including his own *Stones of Venice*)—are very much part of this effort, and find remarkable parallel in Carlyle's *Past and Present* and *The French Revolution.* In *Past and Present* Carlyle, like Browning, portrays the lives of obscure historical figures such as Jocelin of Brakelond or Landlord Edmond. In his accounts of them, he disdains the disembodied history studied by the dilettante and the pedant, which gives no sense of the actuality or the flesh-and-blood existence of their world. In an effort similar to Browning's, Carlyle uses particular detail—words of medieval Latin, commonplace incidents, routines of daily life—to recapture the existential reality of their world.

In his essays, Carlyle continually emphasizes the principle his works demonstrate: that history must give us not philosophy, not parliamentary records, but a sense of how life was actually lived by men. In his essay on Scott, he praises Scott for teaching us

> that the bygone ages of the world were actually filled by living men, not by protocols, state papers, controversies and abstractions of men. Not abstractions were they, not diagrams and theorems; but men, in buff or other coats and breeches, with colour in their cheeks, with passions in their stomach, and the idioms, features, and vitalities of very men.[20]

He then calls for historians to take note of Scott's lesson and exchange philosophy for "direct inspection and embodiment." In his essay on biography, Carlyle again criticizes historians for not giving us acquaintance with our fellow creatures from the past, for not telling us

> how they got along in those old days, suffering and doing; to what extent, and under what circumstances, they resisted the Devil and triumphed over him, or struck their colours to him, and were trodden under foot by him; how, in short, the perennial Battle went, which men name Life. . . .[21]

In his essay on Boswell's *Life of Johnson*, Carlyle praises Boswell for giving us more insight into the history of England than any twenty histories, and then asserts:

> The thing I want to see is not Redbook Lists, and Court Calendars, and Parliamentary Registers, but the LIFE OF MAN in England: what men did, thought, suffered, enjoyed; the form, especially the spirit, of their terrestrial existence, its outward environment, its inward principle; *how* and *what* it was; whence it proceeded, whither it was tending.[22]

In his review of *The French Revolution*, Mill praises Carlyle for doing precisely what Carlyle wanted the historian and the biographer to do: give a real sense of the lives and deeds of his fellow men. He then criticizes several other historians for not doing this, and in his criticisms describes an ideal for history similar to Carlyle's. Here, for example, is Mill's criticism of Hume:

> Does Hume throw his own mind into the mind of an Anglo-Saxon, or an Anglo-Norman? Does any reader feel, after having read Hume's history, that he can now picture to himself what human life was, among the Anglo-Saxons? how an Anglo-Saxon would have acted in any supposable case? what were his joys, his sorrows, his hopes and fears, his ideas and opinions on any of the great and small matters of human interest? . . .

> Or descending from the history of civilization, which in
> Hume's case may have been a subordinate object, to the
> history of political events: did anyone ever gain from
> Hume's history anything like a picture of what may have
> actually been passing, in the minds, say, of Cavaliers or of
> Roundheads during the civil wars? Does anyone feel that
> Hume has made him figure to himself with any precision
> what manner of men these were; how far they were like
> our-selves, how far different; what things they loved and
> hated, and what sort of conception they had formed of the
> things they loved and hated? [23]

The ancients thought history was less valuable than poetry because it was concerned not with the universal but with the accidental and the particular. Mill praises history for that very reason: Carlyle's history, he states, contains exactly that mixture
of the great and the contemptible that we meet in nature.[24]
Mill's judgment reflects a great change in the sense of the location of reality. Because the ancients felt reality was contained
in universals, they felt attention to the accidental was functional only insofar as it implied universal ethical categories.
Mill feels it is accidentals that contain the greatest reality. *On
Liberty* contains a similar emphasis on the importance of the
particular. Just as Mill sees historical reality in the peculiar
character of an epoch, so he asserts that a person becomes valuable in proportion to the development of his individuality.
Mill, like Browning, locates the essence of history and identity
in the particular.

Browning's dramatic monologues give a sense of history
similar to the one Mill desires, but the existential historicism
of his poetry makes great demands on the judging and mythologizing faculties of poet and reader. While it still demands an
evaluative vision, it undermines the validity of all general standards and categories. Each individual must therefore jump
from the trivial particular to the significant universal in every
single act of judgment. Despite his own view of history, Carlyle complained that *The Ring and the Book* was "all made
out of an Old Bailey story that might have been told in ten

lines and only wants forgetting." [25] This tension between the apparent insignificance, even sordidness, of the subject and the elaborateness of its treatment is, however, absolutely essential to Browning's vision. *The Ring and the Book* is Browning's epic, written in twelve books and studded with mythological references. By this implicit comparison to other epics Browning suggests that the act of mythologizing for him begins not with the obvious types but with such sordid and trivial particulars as he chooses. The tension between the particular and the symbolic levels of the poem shows that seeing, judging, and mythologizing are all highly dynamic processes that must continually oscillate between trivial detail and general types.

Matthew Arnold wanted poetry to portray great human actions that appeal to universal human passions, and in his own poetry he sought these actions in myth. Browning chose to seek myth through history. His Andromeda and Perseus, his Adam and Eve are the figures of an obscure Italian murder trial. The statements of history, as Aristotle observes, are not universals but particulars. Neoclassicists distrust history for much the same reason Arnold distrusts Browning: it does not present a governing idea but the world's multitudinousness. The world's multiplicity, which caused Arnold so much anxiety, becomes for Browning the source of its meaning.

In "Henry Purcell," Hopkins announces, "It is the forgèd feature finds me; it is the rehearsal / Of own, of abrúpt sélf there so thrusts on, so throngs the ear." [26] The sonnet suggests the impulse behind much of Hopkins's poetry. Just as he listens to Purcell's music with an ear to his especial originality, an eye to his individual markings and mottlings, so he searches in each created thing for what he calls its "inscape," its distinctive pattern that separates it from anything else. We can see this search in his journals where he describes the inscapes of natural objects in precise scientific detail.

End of March and beginning of April—This is the time to study inscape in the spraying of trees, for the swelling buds carry them to a pitch which the eye could not else

gather—for out of much much more, out of little not
much, out of nothing nothing: in these sprays at all events
there is a new world of inscape. The male ashes are very
boldly jotted with the heads of the bloom which tuft the
outer ends of the branches. The staff of each of these
branches is closely knotted with the places where buds are
or have been, so that it is something like a finger which
has been tied up with string and keeps the marks. They
are in knops of a pair, one on each side, and the knops are
set alternately, at crosses with the knops above and the
knops below, the bud of course is a short smoke-black
pointed nail-head or beak pieced of four lids or nippers.[27]

Hopkins resembles Ruskin in the painstaking accuracy with
which he describes nature. A passage from Ruskin's diary:

Chamouni, June 23.—9 o'clock, morning. There is a
strange effect on Mont Blanc. The Pavillon Hills are
green and clear, with the pearly clearness that foretells
rain; the sky above is fretted with spray of white compact
textured cloud which looks like flakes of dead arborescent
silver. Over the snow, this is concentrated into a cumulus
of the Turner character, not heaped, but laid sloping on
the mountain, silver white at its edge, pale grey in interior; the whole of the snow is cast into shadow by it, and
comes dark against it; especially the lower curve of the
Aiguille du Goûter. But on the summit the cloud is
melted into mist, and what I suppose to be a heavy snow-
storm is falling on the Grand Plateau, and in the hollow
behind the Grands Mulets; into this shower the mountain
retires gradually, and the summit is entirely veiled.[28]

In *Modern Painters,* Ruskin turns this enthusiasm for precise
observation of natural objects into an aesthetic. He makes his
descriptions of the truth of clouds, the truth of earth, the truth
of water, and the truth of vegetation into criteria for judging
the greatness of past artists. A passage from his chapter on the
truth of cirrus clouds suggests how rigorous his demand for
accuracy was.

The edges of the bars of the upper clouds which are turned to the wind, are often the sharpest which the sky shows; no outline whatever of any other kind of cloud, however marked and energetic, ever approaches the delicate decision of these edges. The outline of a black thunder-cloud is striking, from the great energy of the colour or shade of the general mass; but as a line, it is soft and indistinct, compared with the edge of the cirrus in a clear sky with a brisk breeze. On the other hand, the edge of the bar turned away from the wind is always soft, often imperceptible, melting into the blue interstice between it and its next neighbor. Commonly, the sharper one edge is, the softer the other; and the clouds look flat, as if they slipped over each other like the scales of a fish. When both edges are soft, as is always the case when the sky is clear and windless, the cloud looks solid, round, and fleecy.[29]

We have seen the search for aesthetic and moral truth through accurate observation of natural detail in the paintings of the Pre-Raphaelite Brotherhood; *Modern Painters* is the most elaborate Victorian attempt to find aesthetic significance in the accurate observation of things. Hopkins ultimately creates a theology whose starting point is the particularity of natural objects. I will deal with the dynamics of this theology, the process of instress, in the next chapter. Here I only want to establish Hopkins's vision of the world's particularity and multiplicity.

Like Browning, Hopkins sees the universe as composed of particulars, each of which is absolutely distinctive. Although Hopkins's emphasis falls much more on nature than on people, he, like Browning, sees particularity as a dynamic principle. Each thing continually acts out its distinctive identity.

> As kingfishers catch fire, dragonflies draw flame;
>   As tumbled over rim in roundy wells
>   Stones ring; like each tucked string tells, each
>   hung bell's

Bow swung finds tongue to fling out broad its name;
Each mortal thing does one thing and the same:
    Deals out that being indoors each one dwells;
    Selves—goes itself; *myself* it speaks and spells,
Crying *What I do is me: for that I came.*

[p. 90]

The statement each being makes of its particular identity is
unselfconscious; it is merely the result of its being what it is.
In "Henry Purcell," Hopkins uses the metaphor of a bird taking flight for the way in which Purcell reveals his inscape in
his music. Just as the bird in taking off displays the distinctive
white markings under his wings, without the least intention of
identifying himself, so Purcell shows his individuality not in
any effort to do so, which would result in "your damned subjective rot," but while intent on the thought and feeling he is
to express or call out.[30]

Let him oh! with his air of angels then lift me, lay me! only I'll
Have an eye to the sakes of him, quaint moonmarks, to his
    pelted plumage under
Wings: so some great stormfowl, whenever he has walked his
    while

The thunder-purple seabeach plumèd purple-of-thunder,
If a wuthering of his palmy snow-pinions scatter a colossal
    smile
Off him, but meaning motion fans fresh our wits with wonder.

[p. 80]

Grotesque visible forms and speech patterns in Browning
express the inner energy of highly particular beings, which
continually outgrow any classical or static pattern and which
transgress even their own limits. Hopkins conveys a similar
energy by wrenching language so far from its conventional patterns that it becomes a perfectly shaped receptacle of the distinctive energy given off by the object contemplated. He throws
his poems into aggressively bizarre, almost grotesque shapes
that imitate the peculiar energy of the particular. Although he

does not dwell on the grotesque in personalities and natural objects, as does Browning, he does use some of the same linguistic patterns that create Browning's grotesque style. The disjunction of the elements of a perception, for example, reflects a similar insistence on following the individual energy of each element.

To what serves mortal beauty | —dangerous; does dancing blood—the O-seal-that-so | feature, flung prouder form Than Purcell tune lets tread to?

[p. 98]

Yes. Whý do we áll, seeing of a soldier, bless him? bless Our redcoats, our tars? Both these being, the greater part, But frail clay, nay but foul clay. Here it is . . .

[p. 99]

Again like Browning, he gives metaphors so much energy and definition they continually escape their objects to become objects in their own right.

The world is charged with the grandeur of God.
    It will flame out, like shining from shook foil;
    It gathers to a greatness, like the ooze of oil
Crushed.

[p. 66]

Look at the stars! look, look up at the skies!
    O look at all the fire-folk sitting in the air!
    The bright boroughs, the circle-citadels there!
Down in dim woods the diamond delves! the elves'-eyes!
The grey lawns cold where gold, where quickgold lies!

[p. 66]

Here the reader cannot even tell whether each phrase is a metaphor for the starry sky, a metaphor for an object in the preceding phrase, or an independent object in the landscape, each phrase has so much individual energy.

Hopkins insists so aggressively on the particularity of objects partially in reaction to the deindividualizing character of the

modern age. Hopkins sees modern man quickly reducing everything to mud or slime, his symbol for the lack of particularity,
the opposite of inscape.

> Generations have trod, have trod, have trod;
>   And all is seared with trade; bleared, smeared with toil:
>   And wears man's smudge and shares man's smell: the soil
> Is bare now, nor can foot feel, being shod.
>
> [p. 66]

>   We, life's pride and cared-for crown,
>
> Have lost that cheer and charm of earth's past prime:
> Our make and making break, are breaking, down
>   To man's last dust, drain fast towards man's first slime.
>
> [p. 68]

He deplores man's ability to unselve natural objects, to destroy
the particularity that is the mark of God's creation. In his
diary he notes that when he heard the sound of an ash tree
being felled, he "wished to die and not to see the inscapes of
the world destroyed any more" (*J*, p. 230), and in "Binsey
Poplars," he laments that

>   Ten or twelve, only ten or twelve
>   Strokes of havoc únselve
>   The sweet especial scene,
>   Rural scene, a rural scene,
>   Sweet especial rural scene.
>
> [p. 79]

In Hopkins, emphasis upon particularity acts as a form of
pastoral. For Johnson and Reynolds nature approached its
purest, most ideal state when least particular. For Hopkins exactly the opposite is true: nature is most pure when most particular. The destruction modern civilization brings to the inscapes of the world is therefore measured by the distance it
compels between man and nature. Insensitivity to particularity
becomes the measure of man's corruption, of the destruction of
his own inscape. Renewed sensitivity to particularity heals this

corruption and carries man back to "that cheer and charm of earth's past prime." As in Browning, particularity provides a way of reapproaching nature lost to the modern world.

Hopkins is not alone in feeling modern civilization's threat to the individuality of both nature and humanity. Ruskin calls the modern age the age of grey and brown: "We build brown brick walls and wear brown coats." [31] He sees the absolute type of impurity, using terms remarkably like Hopkins's, in "the mud or slime of a damp, over-trodden path, in the outskirts of a manufacturing town"; all its elements are at helpless war with each other, and "destroy reciprocally each other's nature and power, competing and fighting for place at every tread of your foot." [32] He feels, like Hopkins, that awareness of the particularity of nature will not only create better painting but will help abate the dehumanizing, deindividualizing tendencies of modern civilization. Dickens too, has a similar vision of the blear and smear of modern life. The symbols he uses that suggest the destructive potential of life in modern society—the fog in *Bleak House,* the mud in *Our Mutual Friend*—are obfuscating elements that eliminate distinctions, threatening to engulf the lives of all the highly particular characters that populate his novels.

A number of Victorian writers, however, see the danger of modern civilization not in its extinguishing of particularity but in its emphasis of it to create a world that is atomistic. The gathering of large numbers of people into cities, the absence of the social structure that had previously ordered them, and the Darwinian struggle for survival among them—all combined to produce a vision of men as atoms, helplessly colliding with one another. In "The Condition of the Working Class in 1844," Friedrich Engels writes:

> And however much one may be aware that this isolation of the individual, this narrow self-seeking is the fundamental principle of our society everywhere, it is nowhere so shamelessly barefaced, so self-conscious as here in the crowding of the great city. The dissolution of mankind

into monads of which each one has a separate principle,
into the world of atoms, is here carried out to its utmost
extreme.[33]

Dorothy Van Ghent suggests a similar analysis of Dickens's
world.

> Dickens' soliloquizing characters, for all their funniness
> . . . suggest a world of isolated integers, terrifyingly alone
> and unrelated. . . . Perhaps if one could fix on two of the
> most personal aspects of Dickens' technique, one would
> speak of the strange languages he concocts for the solitari-
> ness of soul, and the abruptness of his tempo. His human
> fragments suddenly shock against one another in colli-
> sions like those of Democritus' atoms or of the charged
> particles of modern physics.[34]

At first it may seem that atomism and the dissolution of particularity are opposite threats to human identity, but the dangers each embodies are remarkably similar. In opposite forms
both suggest the loss of that relatedness which defines not only
the social order but individual identity. Both signify the destruction of the social contract, the loss of the individual's
relationship to any whole. Although the atomistic nature of
the modern city makes each individual a law unto himself,
it also makes the individual anonymous, because communication fails, and strangely mechanistic, because each is unable
to do anything but follow the particular drive that propels
him, and propels him into conflict with all else. Ruskin's
description of the mud outside an industrial town, which
obviously reflects the life inside the town, emphasizes precisely this helpless war of elements with each other. For
Ruskin the struggle results in the loss of identity rather than
insularity, but the condition he describes is very similar to that
of which Engels writes. The combination of obfuscating soci-
etal symbols and isolated characters in Dickens's novels suggests that modern society both atomizes individuals and threatens to engulf them in anonymous, smothering social forces. The
dissolution of individuality and the extreme extension of it to

the principle of atomism are opposite ways of stating the destruction modern civilization has brought to individuality as the principle of social relatedness and cohesion it once was.

Although Hopkins emphasizes consciousness of particularity as a response to the destructive potential of modern civilization, he is very aware of the danger of atomism. In "The Probable Future of Metaphysics," an essay written in 1867, he discusses the threat the prevalent atomic, materialistic philosophy of continuity or flux poses to metaphysical speculation. His statement that "to the prevalent philosophy and science nature is a string all the differences in which are really chromatic but certain places in it have become accidentally fixed and the series of fixed points becomes an arbitrary scale" (J, p. 120) describes a number of Victorian philosophies—Darwinism, Benthamism, atomism. Hopkins attacks their denial of the reality of classes, for he thinks this would make impossible any metaphysical speculation or Platonic ideals, which are necessary for Hopkins's conception of God as the patterning force. In opposition to their chromatism, he proposes a diatonism, according to which we would relate all phenomena to certain fixed points at definite distances from each other, much as we relate musical patterns to the scale and the system of harmony it implies.

At first the new Platonism Hopkins calls for in this essay seems diametrically opposed to the entire conception of his poetry. His sense of the unique inscape of every object seems to produce a world of particulars, like Darwin's, without connection to type or species, and to imply the dangers of atomism, since everything is isolated from everything else by its unique inscape. This is not the case, however, because he does not see things as monochrome but as pied, so that each thing derives its peculiar existence, or inscape, from a unique interlocking or interweaving or coincidence of characteristics. He celebrates this piedness of the universe in "Pied Beauty."

> Glory be to God for dappled things—
>> For skies of couple-colour as a brinded cow;
>>> For rose-moles all in stipple upon trout that swim;

Fresh-firecoal chestnut-falls; finches' wings;
  Landscape plotted and pieced—fold, fallow, and plough;
    And áll trádes, their gear and tackle and trim.
All things counter, original, spare, strange;
  Whatever is fickle, freckled (who knows how?)
    With swift, slow; sweet, sour; adazzle, dim;
He fathers-forth whose beauty is past change:
                            Praise him.

                                            [pp. 69–70]

Although the inscape of each object—the stippling of each
trout, the plotting of each landscape—is absolutely peculiar to
it, the qualities themselves—swift, slow, sweet, sour—can be
present in any number of objects. For this reason, the poem
can move from the extreme of concrete particularity—a sky of
couple-colour, a finch's wing—to a generalized description of
it—fickle, freckled, adazzle, dim. J. Hillis Miller sees pattern as
the essence of inscape.[35] Miller's definition, although it places
too much stress on repetition, does point out the pied nature
of the identity of objects in Hopkins's world. They consist not
of unique essences but of unique combinations, nets, or webs
of characteristics. Because objects share characteristics, although
not the patterning of characteristics, the process of instressing
the inscape of a single unique thing throws the poet out toward
instressing other things through metaphor, so that perceiving
a particular inscape necessarily leads to perceiving relationships. This is nowhere better illustrated than in Hopkins's lists
of words. He begins with a word for a single object, such as
"horn." Examining its various aspects gives rise to dozens of
metaphors, thrusting him outward toward the perception of
other objects.

> The various lights under which a horn may be looked
> at have given rise to a vast number of words in language.
> It may be regarded as a projection, a climax, a badge of
> strength, power or vigour, a tapering body, a spiral, a
> wavy object, a bow, a vessel to hold withal or to drink
> from, a smooth hard material not brittle, stony, metallic

or wooden, something sprouting up, something to thrust
or push with, a sign of honour or pride, an instrument of
music, etc. [*J*, p. 4]

His poems proceed in much the same way. In trying to perceive the inscape of one scene or object—a starlight night, for
example—he is pushed toward perceiving other objects re-
sembling aspects of the one before him.

The most profound unity Hopkins's universe, however,
springs not from its piedness but from God. As in Browning,
this unity is found in particularity: the particularity of an object is the stamp of God's creation upon it. God fathers forth
"all things counter, original, spare, strange." God is present in
the universe in his creation of its multiplicity and particularity.
For this reason, Hopkins's poems celebrating this multiplicity
—"Pied Beauty," "As Kingfishers Catch Fire"—end with assertions of God's glory. He whose beauty is past change has created all of the dappled things of the universe. The multitude
of particular incarnations he has created reveals his infinite po-
tentiality. The more various the universe, the more it attests
to his creative power, for

> Christ plays in ten thousand places,
> Lovely in limbs, and lovely in eyes not his
> To the Father through the features of men's faces.
>
> [p. 90]

Thus the more precisely and delicately man apprehends the
world's particularity, the closer he comes to the perception of
its unity in Christ.

Although Hopkins's sense of the unity in the world's multiplicity is theological, whereas Browning's is vitalistic, even in
relation to ethics, their sensitivity to particularity takes a remarkably similar form. Both poets see each element of the universe as propelled by a highly individual life force, which
throws objects, personalities, and the texture of their poetry
itself into aggressively bizarre, often grotesque forms. The
grotesque results from a suspension of necessity, an abolition

of the categories we use to orient our experience. Browning and Hopkins, however, see in this suspension of necessity a resolution to some of the threats many of the early Victorians felt implicit in a sensitivity to particularity. For Tennyson, Arnold, and Carlyle the bond the Romantics had felt joining man to nature had been broken, and they found themselves alone, facing a hostile environment. Particularity implied this new imprisonment in subjectivity and the loss of nature's symbolic potential. Browning and Hopkins transform this sensitivity to particularity into a principle of reintegration of man and nature. They use particularity to portray a world of universal animation in which man approaches nature once more because the same kind of force that creates the oddity of a toadstool or the inscape of a windhover creates the individuality of a Fra Lippo Lippi or the arch-especial spirit of a Henry Purcell.

3

The Good Moment:
The Mastery of Accident

The world composed of mere particulars I have described in the last chapter raised for the Victorians the question of the nature of the knowledge an individual attains from sensation. In a world in which classes, types, ideas are the ultimate reality, the perceiver must merely separate accident from essence in the individual manifestations of ideal types surrounding him. But in a world where accident is essence, the perceiver must determine whether knowledge is limited to the sensation of mere particulars. Can the sensation of particulars give him a knowledge beyond those particulars? Does he experience moments in which he transcends the particulars he senses in perceptions that go beyond them and even persist through time? How does he attain such moments? Can he control them? Both Browning and Hopkins portray an experience in their poetry I would like to call the good moment, in which man does find revelation of a transcendent reality through the particular. The experience resembles and in fact anticipates the epiphany of Joyce or Woolf, in which an intuitive flash suddenly invests some common object with visionary significance. That visionary significance differs for Browning and Hopkins, but the problem the experience reflects and the dynamic by which it is attained are remarkably similar.

Before I turn to Browning and Hopkins, however, I would like to look at the conclusion to *The Renaissance*, where Pater discusses the problem Browning and Hopkins so often portray —the limitations that a world of mere particulars imposes upon individual consciousness. Pater begins the conclusion by constructing an atomistic vision of what we conceive to be our physical life. It consists, Pater asserts, of a temporary combination of natural elements active throughout the universe: calcium, phosphorous, lime. The parts of our body we regard as real, therefore, are merely combinations of forces active in many different places, which will part sooner or later on their way. "That clear, perpetual outline of a face and limb is but an image of ours, under which we group them—a design in a web, the actual threads of which pass out beyond it."

Pater matches this atomistic vision of our physical life with an even more atomistic view of the inward world of thought and feeling, for here change is not gradual but so rapid the mind can barely comprehend it. Our mental life consists of a rush of impressions of external objects, which take flight as soon as they have hit our senses. Furthermore, even these impressions, which at first appear to be cohesive, dissolve upon reflection into a group of sensations of color, shape, and texture. Pater furthermore asserts that these impressions are the impressions of the isolated individual. Each of us is ringed round by a thick wall of personality "through which no real voice has ever pierced on its way to us, or from us to that which we can only conjecture to be without."

We can see in Pater's analysis a paradoxical combination, implicit in impressionism, of extreme scientism, which seeks to observe natural phenomena with increasing precision, and extreme subjectivism, which asserts the uniqueness of individual experience. Pater wants impressions to be at once photographically precise, scientifically analyzable, and subjectively unique. He implies both that we should and that we cannot divine the real character of objects before us. This tension between subjectivism and objectivism is one we have seen throughout our study of the Victorian sensitivity to particularity. It results from the fragmentation of the Romantic understanding of a world we half perceive and half create into a frantic search for the reality of objects and a growingly burdensome conviction of the isolating subjectivity of all experience. Pater does little to resolve this conflict; Browning and Hopkins attain a theological resolution, more by faith than by thought; but its philosophical resolution does not come until the literature of the early twentieth century. Nevertheless, both the scientific and subjectivist aspects of impressionism emphasize a sensitivity to particularity that helps create the peculiar character of post-Romantic poetry.

Pater extends his particularistic sense of objects and impressions to our experience of time itself. After reducing experience to a series of impressions of the individual in isolation, he asserts that these impressions are limited to an instant's duration. Analysis shows us

> that those impressions of the individual mind to which, for each one of us, experience dwindles down, are in perpetual flight; that each of them is limited by time, and that as time is infinitely divisible, each of them is infinitely divisible also; all that is actual in it being a single moment, gone while we try to apprehend it, of which it may ever be more truly said that it has ceased to be than that it is. To such a tremulous wisp constantly re-forming itself on the stream, to a single sharp impression, with a sense in it, a relic more or less fleeting, of such moments gone by, what is real in our life fines itself down.

Here we have the farthest extension of the concept of particularity. The moments of our consciousness are as particular and multitudinous as the objects that shape those moments.

Pater's consciousness of time results naturally from the climate of the age. Time obsessed the Victorians.[1] They had witnessed a collapse of the dimension of eternity within the framework of religious belief, within the philosophical framework of verities and values, and within the social framework of apparently permanent, fixed social and political structure.[2] Time thus came to be experienced increasingly as constant change totally enclosing all of human experience. The new sciences of the age, geology and evolutionary biology, were governed by temporal methodologies. Social thinkers such as Spencer, Marx, and Huxley developed historicist theories of social progress. The extraordinary rate of change and the material progress of the era supported this developing sense of temporal process as the dominant reality. Even the most solid things seemed to be constantly changing.

> The hills are shadows, and they flow
>   From form to form, and nothing stands;
>   They melt like mist, the solid lands,
> Like clouds they shape themselves and go.[3]

At the same time that the barriers of the past were pushed back as never before in geological and historical studies, the rate of change made continuity and identity with the past increasingly difficult to establish. The consciousness of temporal process and the collapse of the beliefs that had been seen as structuring the progress of time combined to create an increasingly radical emphasis upon the moment as the medium of experience. In *The Sense of an Ending* (pp. 24–25), Frank Kermode suggests that when men no longer have a sure sense of the progress of time from creation to apocalypse, they relocate the "end-feeling" in the moment. When they lose confidence that time is progressing toward an end point that will justify and reveal time's meaning and open out onto eternity, they attempt to conceive of such an end as potentially present in every moment. No longer able to sense the end as imminent, they try to make it immanent. The idea of eternity grows personal and psychological.

We can see this personal and psychological conception of eternity in Joyce, in Yeats, in T. S. Eliot, among other twentieth-century writers, but Kermode's theory also offers us an interesting perspective on Pater's philosophy. Pater senses no structure of continuity to time. He surrounds his vision of the moment with a profound sense of death. In the conclusion to *The Renaissance,* he speaks with a constant consciousness of life's awful brevity. He quotes Hugo: "les hommes sont tous condamnés à mort avec des sursis indéfinis." In *Marius the Epicurean,* Marius discovers his philosophy of the moment— the Ideal Now or the New Cyrenaicism—after the death of his best friend. Physically and psychologically in these works, death is an arbitrary end point to experience. Philosophically, it suggests the death of meaningful continuity in time.

Because of this lack of meaning in the natural temporal progress of life, Pater insists that man must create meaning separately in each of the moments of his life by assuming an attitude of passionate intensity. He must burn with a hard, gemlike flame in order to make the most of his moments simply for those moments' sake.

> Every moment some form grows perfect in hand or face; some tone on the hills or the sea is choicer than the rest; some mood of passion or insight or intellectual excitement is irresistibly real and attractive for us,—for that moment only. Not the fruit of experience, but experience itself, is the end. A counted number of pulses only is given to us of a variegated, dramatic life. How may we see in them all that is to be seen in them by the finest senses? How shall we pass most swiftly from point to point, and be present always at the focus where the greatest number of vital forces unite in their purest energy?
>
> To burn always with this hard, gem-like flame, to maintain this ecstasy, is success in life.

Pater's definition of the intense moment directly anticipates the aesthetic moment Wilde and the decadents of the nineties pursued. Observed, as he so often is, from the perspective of the nineties, however, Pater seems much more isolated from the intellectual currents of his century than in fact he is. The differences that separate Pater from his age lie not so much in the ideas he propounds as in his emotional attitudes toward them. He has given up the melancholy search for metaphysical certainty that obsesses the rest of the century to embrace its nominalism. He does not spend time regretting the new relativist spirit of modern thought, but welcomes it and immediately turns his energy toward forming new values that will free our sensibilities to appreciate the details experience presents us.

Pater rejects the pursuit of general knowledge, not only be-

cause he thinks it impossible to attain but because its pursuit
dulls our appreciation for the things that are. It was the effort
to apprehend the absolute—"an effort of sickly thought"—
that Pater asserts saddened the mind of Coleridge and limited
the operation of his poetic gift. The search for abstract truth
saps our energy and impoverishes our perception by mediating
our impressions of objects through preconceived values. "It is
only the roughness of the eye that makes any two persons,
things, situations, seem alike." Thus any failure to apprehend
passionately the unique character of the object before us is
a failure of perception. Pater insists upon an almost utilitarian
equation of objects in terms of the pleasure they provide. His
refusal to make distinctions between "the picture, the landscape, the engaging personality in life or in a book, *La Gio-
conda,* the hills of Carrara, Pico of Mirandola" except in the
unique pleasure each gives [4] recalls Bentham's comparison of
poetry with a game of pushpin; but Pater means his equation
to lead not to quantitative measurement but rather to a clear-
ing of the sensibilities so that we can experience our impressions as fully and immediately as possible.

The value Pater places upon intensity and immediacy of
experience recalls the poems of Rossetti I discussed in the first
chapter. Pater gives the Pre-Raphaelite quest for intensity the
philosophically particularist perspective it implies. He transforms sensitivity to detail from a way of defining an aesthetic
state to an embodiment of both an epistemology and the ethical stance that epistemology requires.

In the light of Pater's development of Pre-Raphaelite
values, it is interesting to observe Rossetti's own poetic development. In *The House of Life,* most of which was written in
the late sixties and early seventies, about twenty years after
the poems we have analyzed, Rossetti extends his particularist
understanding of the sensation of objects to our experience of
time itself, in a way similar to Pater's. The main theme of *The
House of Life* is mutability. It portrays experience as a succession of ephemeral moments, which dissolve even as we
try to apprehend them. Rossetti's response to the transitori-
ness of experience, much like Pater's, is a demand for inten-

sity. Man can save his moments from the devouring power of time only by an intense imaginative effort both in living them and in memorializing them in art. A sonnet presents and preserves a single exalting moment.

> A Sonnet is a moment's monument,—
>> Memorial from the Soul's eternity
>> To one dead deathless hour. Look that it be,
> Whether for lustral rite or dire portent,
> Of its own arduous fulness reverent:
>> Carve it in ivory or in ebony,
>> As Day or Night may rule; and let Time see
> Its flowering crest impearled and orient.

To combat the power of time, the poet must give his poem the "arduous fulness" of the experience itself. Whether the moment be dedicated to good or evil, "lustral rite or dire portent," is unimportant; the only value is intense realization.

But despite his sense of the particularity of the moment's experience, Rossetti's sonnets rarely contain poetic particularity. With a few exceptions such as "Silent Noon," or "Youth's Spring Tribute," they obscure references to concrete events. They seem distant from whatever incident inspired them. Rossetti constantly uses personifications, abstractions, and elaborately wrought metaphors to portray events of which he gives only the most tenuous outline. By those poetic devices he gives a hardness, a monumental, emblematic quality, like the frieze on a Grecian vase, to fleeting experiences and states of feeling. In *The House of Life*, unlike his earlier lyrics, Rossetti seeks an escape from particularity by transforming experience to artistic convention. His lovers burn with a hard, gemlike flame, but his poetry stills its flickering so that the flame seems carved in marble. He obscures the particularity of the moment in order to transcend it, to make it infinite.

In Browning's poetry, however, portrayals of the moment's experience refuse to qualify its particularity. Like Pater, Browning sees the moment as the medium of the creation and experience of the self. Character after character in Browning's world reveals and commits himself in a moment's deed. Childe

Roland, the lovers in "In a Gondola" or "The Last Ride
Together," Constance, Norbert, and the Queen in "In a Balcony" are named and known by a single moment of commitment, while the worst failures of Browning's world, such as the
lovers of "The Statue and the Bust," "Dîs Aliter Visum," or
"Youth and Art," are those who fail to seize their moment and
commit themselves to it. And once the moment has come in
which the soul has declared and defined itself by the thing
it does, events are insignificant. Browning's poems portraying
the moments of commitment are curiously truncated. The
poems end with the characters' assertion of commitment; the
progress of events is never completed. Although we can anticipate how the stories will end, Browning never tells us what
happens after Childe Roland blows his horn, after the lovers
in "In a Gondola" are surprised, or after the guard enters in
"In a Balcony." Each of the characters has committed an act
that validates his whole life, and any event after that, despite
its consequences, would not affect that moment or that identity.

In creating this tension between the subjective moment and
the objective structure of events, Browning is redefining the
relationship of the self to time. The objective continuities of
time—the progress of events—do not have as much importance in defining the self as the subjective moment. Much as
Pater sees significance not in the progress of life from birth
to death but in moments of heightened perception, so Browning sees the self defined not by the events of its life but by its
moments of assertion and commitment, by "the rare flashes of
momentary conviction that come and go in the habitual dusk
and doubt of one's life." [5]

The poem "Now," written toward the end of his life, states
this conviction that shapes so much of his earlier poetry.

> Out of your whole life give but a moment!
> All of your life that has gone before,
> All to come after it,—so you ignore,
> So you make perfect the present,—condense,

> In a rapture of rage, for perfection's endowment,
> Thought and feeling and soul and sense—
> Merged in a moment . . .

In "The School of Giorgione," Pater defines an ideal for poetry similar to the ideal for life that Browning asserts in "Now."

> Now it is part of the ideality of the highest sort of dramatic poetry, that it presents us with a kind of profoundly significant and animated instants, a mere gesture, a look, a smile, perhaps—some brief and wholly concrete moment—into which, however, all the motives, all the interests and effects of a long history, have condensed themselves, and which seem to absorb past and future in an intense consciousness of the present.[6]

Browning's choice of the dramatic monologue as the principle form of his poetry reflects this vision both of life and of art. The poet can reveal the meaning of a man's life if he can catch him at one of those moments of crisis which "absorb past and future in an intense consciousness of the present." It may be the moment of death, as in "The Bishop Orders His Tomb at Saint Praxed's Church" or perhaps the moment of sudden discovery, as in "Mr. Sludge, 'The Medium' " or "Fra Lippo Lippi," but whenever it occurs, it will be a moment when a man's inner power shows itself in its most essential form, as the light in Mediterranean phares, in the words Browning uses to describe his own poetry, "only after a weary interval leaps out, for a moment, from the one narrow chink, and then goes on with the blind wall between it and you." [7]

Browning's vision of the particular moment as the medium in which man creates himself leads to the problem of how the moment attains a continuity beyond itself, how a good moment can become an infinite moment. "Meeting at Night" describes one of these good moments, in which the banality of normal consciousness disappears to create an instant's recognition and intimacy.

The gray sea and the long black land;
And the yellow half-moon large and low;
And the startled little waves that leap
In fiery ringlets from their sleep,
As I gain the cove with pushing prow,
And quench its speed i' the slushy sand.

Then a mile of warm sea-scented beach;
Three fields to cross till a farm appears;
A tap at the pane, the quick sharp scratch
And blue spurt of a lighted match,
And a voice less loud, through its joys and fears,
Than two hearts beating each to each!

Browning gives the moment its extraordinary intensity through the particularity of the images he uses. The images get more precise as the lovers get closer together. The sharpness of detail in the tap at the pane and the scratch and spurt of the match conveys an intensity of vision like the intensity of communion between the lovers and the minuteness of the images suggests a closeness to eye and ear that conveys the intimacy of the experience. At the same time, however, this very minuteness gives the images a fragility that implies the briefness of the moment. It passes quickly, leaving little that endures. The companion poem to "Meeting at Night," "Parting at Morning," suggests the impossibility of fixing the moment's experience, no matter how intense.

Round the cape of a sudden came the sea,
And the sun looked over the mountain's rim:
And straight was a path of gold for him,
And the need of a world of men for me.

"Two in the Campagna" portrays the experience of a man trying to grasp hold of such a good moment. The speaker yearns for a perfect union with his love, but he can only catch a glimpse of its possibility in a moment's closeness, gone even while he tries to apprehend it.

I would I could adopt your will,
See with your eyes, and set my heart

Beating by yours, and drink my fill
  At your soul's springs,—your part my part
In life, for good and ill.

No. I yearn upward, touch you close,
  Then stand away. I kiss your cheek,
Catch your soul's warmth,—I pluck the rose
  And love it more than tongue can speak—
Then the good minute goes.

Already how am I so far
  Out of that minute?

The lovers' difficulty in finding and preserving intimacy stands in contrast to the boundlessness, openness, and vitality of the campagna in which the poem is set. Nature possesses a freedom and fertility the lovers fail to attain.

The champaign with its endless fleece
  Of feathery grasses everywhere!
Silence and passion, joy and peace,
  An everlasting wash of air—
Rome's ghost since her decease.

Such life here, through such lengths of hours,
  Such miracles performed in play,
Such primal naked forms of flowers,
  Such letting nature have her way
While heaven looks from its towers!

The lover tries to understand the reason for his failure but cannot. As in his experience of love, he catches a glimpse of what the realization might be, but when he tries to grasp hold of it, he loses it. His eye wanders over the landscape, tantalized by minute, seemingly irrelevant detail, perhaps those very details his eyes were resting upon when he felt on the verge of understanding, and which he hopes now might provide the key to the insight which has eluded him.

Help me to hold it! First it left
  The yellowing fennel, run to seed
There, branching from the brickwork's cleft,

> Some old tomb's ruin: yonder weed
> Took up the floating weft,
>
> Where one small orange cup amassed
>   Five beetles,—blind and green they grope
> Among the honey-meal: and last,
>   Everywhere on the grassy slope
> I traced it. Hold it fast!

The way the speaker uses detail suggests much about the process of perception. The multiplicity and particularity of the details that present themselves to his consciousness show the number and diversity, the sheer multitudinousness, of phenomena composing the landscape we live in, and make evident the difficulty of integrating all the elements of a moment's experience into a single realization. In addition, the contrast between the details the speaker fastens upon and the boundlessness of the landscape suggests the relationship between the moments in which the speaker glimpses insight or love and the vast quantity of experience surrounding those moments. They seem as minutely particular as the details of the landscape and as lost in the expanse of the whole. The subject of the poem is the speaker's knowledge of his finiteness despite his desire for infinity. The contrast between the particularity and the vastness of the landscape is one of Browning's ways of dramatizing this experience.

The details also help depict the relationship of sensation to perception. In the stanza quoted above, the speaker is trying to bring together his sensation of particular details with a thought he almost grasped, but for all his efforts, the two remain disjunct. Although the details suggest a sensuality that might be one way of attaining the unity he seeks, the speaker nevertheless fails to catch hold of the insight he is searching for by looking at the objects surrounding him, and immediately after these stanzas, his train of thought wanders off in yet another direction, leaving his impressions of the landscape behind as images only tenuously connected with the progress of his reflections. Browning thus manages to suggest a problematic relation between sensation and thought: while the

whole of an experience encompasses both, the two often fail
to have any congruity. Objects that have little or no connection with the conscious train of our thought impress themselves upon our sensations and acquire a life of their own,
interrupting and qualifying our perceptions. The effect is very
much like that of Alain Resnais's movie, *Last Year at Mar-
ienbad*. Resnais's cinematic technique offers us a succession
of images that have little connection with the plot of the
movie but acquire a mysterious life of their own, so that the
experience the movie presents us consists just as much of these
inessential, strangely forceful impressions of objects as of the
relationships between the characters. In watching the movie,
we feel if we could penetrate the meaning of these objects, we
could solve the mystery of what happened last year at Marien-
bad, just as the speaker of "Two in the Campagna" feels he
could discover the reason for his failure if he could understand the landscape around him, but we possess only the
images and half-articulated intuitions of a harmony now lost
between recognition and sensation.

Browning sometimes uses particularity in his dramatic monologues to express very subtly this noncongruity between sensation and thought. "Count Gismond," for example, has
stirred much critical controversy, and this controversy centers
largely on the impact of a few details upon our acceptance of
the rest of the speaker's narrative.[8] In the poem, a lady relates
the story of a fight between one knight, Count Gauthier, and
her present husband, Count Gismond, over her innocence. On
the day she had been chosen queen of a tournament, Gauthier
publicly accused her of having slept with him. Gismond rose
to defend her honor, killed Gauthier, and then asked her to
marry him. The lady tells her story in a simple and pious
tone: she was the wronged defenseless innocent; Gismond was
God's champion. In her narrative, however, she recalls images
which clash with the tone of the rest of her story.

> Did I not watch him while he let
>   His armorer just brace his greaves,
> Rivet his hauberk, on the fret

> The while! His feet ... my memory leaves
> No least stamp out, nor how anon
> He pulled his ringing gauntlets on.
> . . . .
> Over my head his arm he flung
>   Against the world; and scarce I felt
> His sword (that dripped by me and swung)
>   A little shifted in his belt:
> For he began to say the while
> How South our home lay many a mile.

The images that have imprinted themselves on her memory and that she recalls with a vivid delight are violent and, in the case of the dripping sword, even phallic. A number of readers have seen these images as evidence of the lady's guilt. But the poem does not give us enough information to tell what the real events of the story are, and the many ambiguities Browning suggests about the action are much more important than the determination of the lady's guilt or innocence. The lady and the critics ask us to split absolute guilt and innocence, but the poem asks us to reject this dichotomy and uses its ambiguities to suggest that neither guilt nor innocence is necessarily a pure state. The lady tries to mythologize her experience as the story of God's champion defending wronged innocence, but the images that imprint themselves on her memory reveal a vivid delight in physical combat, which shows that the way she presents herself reflects only a partial sense of her experience. The story, nevertheless, reveals a will for piety and a justification for doing wrong in suffering.

> What says the body when they spring
> Some monstrous torture-engine's whole
> Strength on it? No more says the soul.

Attempts to delimit the significance of the situation, to see the characters as representing either pure guilt or innocence, must fail because of the multifaceted nature of consciousness and the ambiguity of lived experience. It is particularity that

Browning uses to suggest this disjunction between elements of experience.

At first this use of heightened consciousness of sensuous detail at moments of crisis may seem similar to Rossetti's, but the two are really quite different. Although the details Rossetti uses have little connection with his characters' conscious trains of thought, they increase our sense of the emotional unity of the experience. They act as receptacles for its power rather than sensations that acquire their own being and take the experiencer and reader in a different direction from the discursive one of the story. For Rossetti, detail conveys the intensity and immediacy of experience; for Browning, it adds an entirely new dimension to experience. Nor is Browning's use of detail merely ironic. The details in "Count Gismond" do not entirely discredit the lady's story; they rather show it to be a partial sense of the total experience. Browning uses detail to suggest the disjunction and particularity both of our moments of experience and of the elements within those moments.

Given the way he depicts the moment, the problem becomes how man can find a unity and a continuity in those moments. "By the Fireside" portrays what Browning calls an infinite moment, a moment that escapes the boundaries of time and space to give one who experiences it a revelation that will shape his entire life. In the poem, the speaker muses on the walk through the Italian countryside he and his wife took that confirmed their love. The speaker describes the landscape with a sense of its boundlessness, its multiplicity, and its particularity similar to that in "Two in the Campagna."

> Look at the ruined chapel again
>   Half-way up in the Alpine gorge!
> Is that a tower, I point you plain,
>   Or is it a mill, or an iron forge
> Breaks solitude in vain?
>
> A turn, and we stand in the heart of things;
>   The woods are round us, heaped and dim;
> From slab to slab it slips and springs,

The thread of water single and slim,
Through the ravage some torrent brings!

Does it feed the little lake below?
    That speck of white just on its marge
Is Pella; see, in the evening-glow,
    How sharp the silver spear-heads charge
When Alp meets heaven in snow!

On our other side is the straight-up rock;
    And a path is kept 'twixt the gorge and it
By boulder-stones where lichens mock
    The marks on a moth, and small ferns fit
Their teeth to the polished block.

Oh, the sense of the yellow mountain-flowers,
    And the thorny balls, each three in one,
The chestnuts throw on our path in showers!
    For the drop of the woodland's fruit's begun,
These early November hours,

That crimson the creeper's leaf across
    Like a splash of blood, intense, abrupt,
O'er a shield else gold from rim to boss,
    And lay it for show on the fairy-cupped
Elf-needled mat of moss,

By the rose-flesh mushrooms, undivulged
    Last evening-nay, in to-day's first dew
Yon sudden coral nipple bulged,
    Where a freaked, fawn-colored, flaky crew
Of toad-stools peep indulged.

And yonder, at foot of the fronting ridge
    That takes the turn to a range beyond,
Is the chapel reached by the one-arched bridge
    Where the water is stopped in a stagnant pond
Danced over by the midge.

Despite the independence of each object in the landscape,
they come together here in a miraculous harmony that pro-

duces a good moment, creating a new intimacy between the
lovers.

> We stoop and look in through the grate,
>   See the little porch and rustic door,
> Read duly the dead builder's date;
>   Then cross the bridge we crossed before,
> Take the path again—but wait!
>
> Oh moment, one and infinite!
>   The water slips o'er stock and stone;
> The West is tender, hardly bright:
>   How gray at once is the evening grown—
> One star, its crysolite!
> . . . .
> A moment after, and hands unseen
>   Were hanging the night around us fast;
> But we knew that a bar was broken between
>   Life and life: we were mixed at last
> In spite of the mortal screen.

A number of readers have criticized the poem for the random-
ness and insignificance of the details made to carry the burden
of the emotion of the whole. They feel the emotion is not
gotten out of the details clearly enough for them to create the
feeling that is the poem's central revelation.[9] Yet the mys-
teriousness of the connection between the elements of perception and the realization they bring is essential to the experience the poem portrays. It presents a recognition that
comes without will or even anticipation, like an act of grace
and whose content resists rational definition. The poem is
true to that kind of experience which can only be articulated
by recollecting the combination of details that surround it,
though the details themselves fail to declare their significance.

The details Browning selects, however, do suggest a vitalistic harmony with nature similar to that in "An Englishman
in Italy." Browning includes details ranging from the most
primitive forms of life—ferns, moss, mushrooms—to the hu-

man, even religious scene of the chapel. The peculiar energies of all of those forms of life unite to create a natural harmony in which man seems to merge back into nature. This, in fact, is the harmony the lovers intuit and become part of in a way that unites them with each other as well.

> The forests had done it; there they stood;
>   We caught for a moment the powers at play:
> They had mingled us so, for once and good.

Unlike the lovers of "Two in the Campagna," the lovers here attain a unity with nature's vitality and openness.

Yet none of the elements in this unity loses its particularity. In fact, the unity springs from and depends upon its background of multiplicity. "Abt Vogler" provides a good analogy for the way in which this happens. The poem portrays a momentary revelation of God Abt Vogler experiences while extemporizing a composition upon his organ. In building the structure of his composition, Abt Vogler calls upon different sounds to come together and part. Each note he uses is merely itself, but from the combination springs the harmony and revelation of the piece of music. He uses the image of a chord: from three distinct sounds issues not a fourth sound but a star. Yet the chord depends upon and includes each of the individual sounds that create it. The thoughts and impressions of the landscape in "By the Fireside" come together in a similar way. From a combination of elements that remain distinct springs an almost musical harmony and communion, which can persist through time past the moment of its happening.

The central subject of "By the Fireside" is this persistence through time. The poem's time structure is extremely complex. The poem portrays a man looking forward to a future point in old age when he will recollect the past, his present anticipation of what his future imagination of the past will be. One critic has called the poem "anti-romantic" because its real center is not its lyrical climax, but the diffusion of that climax over time.[10] By its time structure, the poem creates a union of past, present, and future which is the psychological equivalent of infinity.

The infinite moment is Browning's solution to the problem that has concerned nineteenth- and twentieth-century writers to an almost obsessive degree: how the qualities of continuity and unity can arise out of an experience that is a temporal succession of discontinuous, disparate moments. Writers have solved this problem a number of ways. One is by extending the moment back in time through memory and forward through anticipation and desire, so that one moment or one day can encompass a whole life as it does in Virginia Woolf's *Mrs. Dalloway* or James Joyce's *Ulysses*. Another is by repeated recollection of particular past moments, such as we find in Wordsworth or in Browning, or of course in Proust. By this recollection man creates a dynamic interpenetration of past, present, and future, such as we see in *A la Recherche du Temps Perdu,* in Browning's "By the Fireside," or in Wordsworth's "Tintern Abbey," which gives the moment an aspect of eternity in time. Wordsworth finds this recollection and continuity fairly easy to attain. Moments of revelation in *The Prelude* come freely to the poet, and he can freely return to them for renovation and recreation. For Proust, this sense of ease has disappeared. The past is fugitive, held captive in a particular past sensation—the taste of a morsel of petite madeleine soaked in tea—that we recapture only when we stumble upon it by accident. For Browning, too, this sense of ease has disappeared because, like Proust, he has radically reduced the sense of continuity of experience through his emphasis on the particularity of our moments of consciousness. They are not merely instants of time but aggressively particular moments whose insights he feels no assurance he can maintain.

The force that enables man to make the leap out of the particular in which his experience is confined is intensity. A vast gap exists between the finiteness of our experience and the infinity we desire; a gap that can only be jumped by energy. Man must throw himself entirely into the particular moment, with all the energy he possesses, like the lovers in "The Last Ride Together": he must burn with a hard gemlike flame, trust that the instant will be made eternity. Then man's intensity will call forth an answering act of grace that will make the moment infinite. In "By the Fireside," the intensity of the man's love calls forth an answering love and generosity in the woman and an answering grace in the forests around them. In "Saul," David's intensity of love for Saul brings about the final revelation of God's infinite love in Christ that forms the last ecstatic section of the poem. In "Abt Vogler," the intensity of Vogler's desire for beauty brings an answering gift from heaven.

> And the emulous heaven yearned down, made effort to
>   reach the earth,
> As the earth had done her best, in my passion, to scale
>   the sky.

The infinity of such a moment can be the transcendence of the boundaries that separate people, as in "By the Fireside," or in the revelation of a religious truth usually denied in the finiteness of our experience, as in "Saul" or "Abt Vogler." The infinite moment can take place in the area of love, art, or religion, but wherever it occurs, it is the intensity of man's striving, the force of his energy and love, that enables him to transcend the particular. Yet this energy alone does not complete the act. That toward which man directs this energy, whether it be another person or God, must reach out with an answering act of grace and love.

Browning's similarity to Kierkegaard and modern existentialists has often been remarked.[11] Like Browning, Kierkegaard creates an ethics of feeling in which the truth of religious and moral values is only apprehended through a passionate subjective commitment, a leap of faith, which issues not just in belief but in action. For Kierkegaard, as for Browning, the defining reality of a man's life is the instant of private commitment, and man's perfection is measured by the intensity of the energy, of that commitment. Browning's close resemblance to Kierkegaard and modern existentialists stems from their common apprehension of a nineteenth-century problem—the growing conviction of man's inability to ascertain universal religious and moral truths objectively through reason and a parallel conviction of the independent reality of each man's experience. To preserve religious and moral values in the face of these convictions, to avoid either aestheticism or skepticism, it became necessary to create an ethics and a religion that admitted the objective uncertainty and the private reality in which we live and that found meaning through the only certainty that remained, the intensity of individual experience. Existentialism is the ultimate religious consequence of empiricism. If the source of knowledge is individual experience, the source of religious and moral value ultimately becomes individual experience as well, and its only standard is intensity. The connection between particular and general can no longer be provided by reason, but only by intuition, emotion, faith, intensity. Modern existentialists see this intensity as its own justification in the face of an absurd world which offers no support to man's values, and Browning occasionally seems to approach this attitude, in poems like "Childe Roland." But more often Browning, like Kierkegaard, sees intensity of commitment creating an answering revelation from God.

Browning is not alone among the Victorians in his assertion that intensity is the quality in life that makes possible whatever moral revelations life has to offer. Although writers of the aesthetic movement such as Rossetti and Pater felt themselves revolutionary in asserting the value of intensity as the way of making our perceptions as full as possible, their attitudes derive rather directly from earlier Victorian religious beliefs. The destruction that science, the higher criticism, and various logical creeds such as utilitarianism and Malthusian economics brought to religious belief led to a lack of faith in reason, even a fear of it, and a renewed assertion of emotional intensity as the foundation of religion, an assertion that was supported by the optimism and sense of progress of the era. The evangelical movement, whose attitudes appear in slightly mutated forms in Carlyle and Tennyson, claimed for the foundation of belief the authority of feeling. To all perplexing

questions, wrote Tennyson, "the heart / Stood up and an-
swered 'I have felt.' "

As the object of Victorian intensity and aspiration grew
increasingly distant, intensity became more a value in itself.
Browning's heroes, Tennyson's Ulysses, George Eliot's Doro-
thea Brooke—all burn with an intensity of feeling whose goal
is only vaguely defined.[12] The aesthetic movement adopted
this prevailing emotional attitude and dissociated it from any
goal beyond experience itself. Browning does not make this
dissociation, but he brings to his belief in intensity a radically
particularist perspective toward time and consciousness that
demands a leap of faith to pass beyond the individual moment's experience.

In his intensity, however, man must always maintain a
sense of the moment's particularity. The attempt to fixate the
particular leads to a morbidity like that in Tennyson's *Maud*,
in which a character imposes a weight upon a detail that it
cannot carry. Browning presents a number of his characters
doing precisely this. In "Cristina," for example, the speaker
thinks that a stray glance the Spanish queen, Maria Cristina,
throws in his direction indicates the rushing together of their
souls in a way that will shape the rest of his life. The poem is
a parody of the good moment of "By the Fireside," the imagination of enormous significance in a trivial particular.
"Porphyria's Lover" portrays a similar instance of a man who
attributes disproportionate significance to a single moment.
The speaker thinks that Porphyria's leaving a party to visit
him is evidence that she worships him. Possessed by an over-
whelming desire to preserve the moment in which he rests his
head on her shoulder and sorry she cannot preserve its truth
in the way he can, he strangles her. In both poems, the speakers become imprisoned in the particular. Cristina's glance
does not act as the spark to a sustained communion, as does
the moment between the lovers in "By the Fireside," but becomes a morbid fixation, and the attempt of Porphyria's lover
to preserve the moment results in murder, imprisoning rather
than liberating the couple in the moment's act.

The line between this fixation in the particular and the kind of commitment to the particular we have seen in "By the Fireside" or "The Last Ride Together" is a difficult one to draw, but the essential difference arises from an acceptance of the process of life and the vitalism of experience. Particularity is a dynamic principle for Browning; the grotesque, as we have seen, is a form of energy. Determination to fixate the particular, which leads to the morbid imprisonment of Cristina's and Porphyria's lovers, is an evil in Browning's world because precisely like the failure of commitment, it refuses to embrace that energy. In *Lord Jim,* Stein tells Marlowe, "to the destructive element submit yourself, and with the exertions of your hands and feet in the water make the deep, deep sea keep you up." Particularity can be a destructive element for Browning, but only by submitting himself to it can man transcend it. Browning once wrote to Ruskin that the task of poetry was "putting the infinite within the finite," but man can do this only by embracing the finite with all his energy and letting it carry him up.

An old lay brother who had been with Hopkins at Stonyhurst recalled that one of the poet's special delights was to run out on the path from the seminary to the college immediately after a shower and crouch down to gaze at the crushed quartz glittering as the sun came out again. "Ay, a strange yoong man," the old brother remarked, "crouching down that gate to stare at some wet sand. A fair natural 'e seemed to us, that Mr. 'opkins" (*J,* p. 408). The story bears an uncanny resemblance to the many anecdotes about Tennyson's sensitivity to detail, but Hopkins changes this vision of crushed quartz among grains of sand or a dragonfly on a wild flower into a sacrament. His poetry sanctifies Browning's good moment, transforming an intense vision of particulars into an epiphany that reveals the reality of Christ.

As the foundation for his vision, Hopkins has a sense of consciousness very similar to that of Pater, who tutored him at Oxford. For Hopkins, man is the most particular, the most determined and distinctive created being. He is, in Hopkins's own language, more highly selved than anything in the world. As a result, a man's sense of what it is to be himself is something absolutely particular, which can never be felt by someone else. When Hopkins considers the "taste of himself,' " he finds it is

> more distinctive than the taste of ale or alum, more distinctive than the smell of walnutleaf or camphor, and is incommunicable by any means to another man (as when I was a child I used to ask myself: What must it be to be someone else?). Nothing else in nature comes near this unspeakable stress of pitch, distinctiveness, and selving, this selfbeing of my own. Nothing explains it or resembles it, except so far as this, that other men to themselves have the same feeling. . . . . But to me there is no resemblance: searching nature I taste *self* but at one tankard, that of my own being.[13]

Although the emphasis and the implications are different, the same idea is central to Pater's conclusion to *The Renaissance.* For Pater, "the whole scope of observation is dwarfed into the narrow chamber of the individual mind." "That thick wall of personality" which for Pater surrounds experience is Hopkins's taste of his inmost self, which, when compared with anything else, makes all things "rebuff me with blank unlikeness."

This conviction of the absolute subjectivity of man's sense of self often awakes, as it does for Pater, a parallel sense of the subjectivity of man's impressions of external objects. Hopkins's early poems on perspective, such as the following one written in 1864 and found in an early diary, explore this problem.

> It was a hard thing to undo this knot.
> The rainbow shines, but only in the thought
> Of him that looks. Yet not in that alone,
> For who makes rainbows by invention?

And many standing round a waterfall
See one bow each, yet not the same to all,
But each hand's breadth further than the next.
The sun on falling waters writes the text
Which yet is in the eye or in the thought.
It was a hard thing to undo this knot.

[pp. 129–130]

Hopkins finds it difficult to reconcile the paradox that we know the objective existence of natural objects through our subjective impressions of them, which differ from one beholder to another. Our knowledge is "special-general"; we can approach the being of other objects only through our particular visions of them. Yet Hopkins is sure that reality does not consist solely in subjective impressions, "for who makes rainbows by invention?" Particular impressions, however paradoxically, do reveal the object, and we can lead other people to our own visions. In a sonnet written to Oxford in the following year, Hopkins presents his vision of the chapel, one which he creates from a very peculiar angle and manipulates by moving his eye, but which he invites others to share or imagines others indeed may have shared.

Thus, I come underneath this chapel-side,
So that the mason's levels, courses, all
The vigorous horizontals, each way fall
In bows above my head, as falsified
By visual compulsion, till I hide
The steep-up roof at last behind the small
Eclipsing parapet; yet above the wall
The sumptuous ridge-crest leave to poise and ride.
None besides me this bye-ways beauty try.
Or if they try it, I am happier then:
The shapen flags and drillèd holes of sky,
Just seen, may be to many unknown men
The one peculiar of their pleasured eye,
And I have only set the same to pen.

The conviction of the uniqueness of personal vision Hopkins shares with Pater does not lead to the same reduction of experience to a succession of fragmentary impressions that have no reality other than themselves. Despite the peculiarity of your own vision, it is possible to approach the being of other objects through your impressions of them; this perception Hopkins calls instress.

Instress actually has two distinct but closely related meanings in Hopkins. First, it is the power or energy that holds a thing together and makes its individual distinctiveness a dynamic force.

> But such a lovely damasking in the sky as today I never felt before. The blue was charged with simple instress, the higher, zenith sky earnest and frowning, lower more light and sweet. [*J.* p. 207]

> To Westminster Abbey, where I went round the cloisters . . . took in the beautiful paired triforium-arcade with cinqfoiled wheels riding the arches (there is a simplicity of instress in the cinqfoil). [*J,* p. 257]

More commonly, however, instress means the apprehension of the actuality or the essence, the individual distinctiveness or inscape, of an object.

> the castle ruins, which crown the hill, were punched out in arches and half arches by bright breaks and eyelets of daylight. We went up to the castle but not in: standing before the gateway I had an instress which only the true old work gives from the strong and noble inscape of the pointearch. [*J,* p. 263]

> Then near Bishopsteignton from a hilltop I looked into a lovely comb that gave me the instress of *Weeping Winifred,* which all the west country seems to me to have: soft maroon or rosy cocoa-dust-coloured handkerchiefs of ploughfields, sometimes delicately combed with rows of green, their hedges bending in flowing outlines and now

misted a little by the beginning of twilight ran down
into it upon the shoulders of the hills; in the bottom
crooked rows of rich tall elms, foreshortened by position, wound through it: some cornfields were still being
carried. [*J*, p. 250]

There is a certain paradox in this twofold meaning Hopkins gives the concept of instress. Its first meaning implies
what Hopkins himself is sure of, the origin of an impression
in the individual distinctiveness of the object itself. Instress
in the second sense would then be an activization, in the form
of a perception, of this dynamic essence, and this is in fact
how Hopkins most often uses the term. Instress seems to have
a double existence, both in the object and in the perceiver, as
here where he describes a lunar halo:

I could not but strongly feel in my fancy the odd instress
of this, the moon leaning on her side, as if fallen back, in
the cheerful light floor within the ring, after with magical
rightness and success tracing round her the ring the
steady copy of her own outline. [*J*, p. 218]

The frequent ambiguity of Hopkins's location of the term is
functional in that it identifies the force in the object and in
the perception as the same. But instress often comes danger-
ously close to an impression that can only be articulated in
terms of subjective emotions not inherent in the object.

The comet—I have seen it at bedtime in the west, with
head to the ground, white, a soft well-shaped tail, not big:
I felt a certain awe and instress, a feeling of strangeness,
flight (it hangs like a shuttlecock at the height, before it
falls), and of threatening. [*J*, p. 249]

The element that differentiates Hopkins's concept of instress
from impression and enables him to resolve the paradox inherent in the double location he gives it is a dynamic thrust,
an intensity of address of the perceiver toward the object. It
is this intensity that enables the viewer to go beyond a merely
subjective impression to a perception of the essence of the

object. It is as if the viewer's intensity makes the individual
pattern of the object into a dynamic communicative force.

> What you look hard at seems to look hard at you,
> hence the true and the false instress of nature. One day
> early in March when long streamers were rising over
> Kemble End one large flake loop-shaped, not a streamer
> but belonging to the string, moving too slowly to be seen,
> seemed to cap and fill the zenith with a white shire of
> cloud. I looked up at it till the tall height and the beauty
> of the scaping—regularly curled knots springing if I
> remember from fine stems, like foliation in wood or stone
> —had strongly grown on me. [*J*, p. 204]

The viewer's intensity—his looking hard—makes the inscape
of the object at which he is looking dynamic so that the object
seems to look hard at him. He thereby creates a communication of particularities—an instress of inscape received through
his own inscape—which transcends separateness into unity.

This element of dynamic interaction between the perceived
and the perceiver separates Hopkins's sense of perception from
Pater's. Like Pater, Hopkins feels we must perceive with all
the delicacy of differentiation and all the intensity we can. For
Pater, however, intensity has its end only in a richer flux of
impressions, which have their reality only in the subjectivity
of the perceiver. For Hopkins, intensity enables man to go beyond subjective impressions to apprehend the inscape of another object, though it must be an extremely particular inscape. As for Browning, intensity makes possible the leap
from the particular. For this reason, Hopkins often begins his
poems with a thrust of energy out toward his subject.

I caught this morning morning's minion

Look at the stars! look, look up at the skies!

I walk, I lift up, I lift up heart, eyes,
Down all that glory in the heavens to glean our Saviour

Perception, in fact, demands this thrust of energy. As Hopkins says of Christ in "The Wreck of the Deutschland,"

> Since, tho' he is under the world's splendour and wonder,
>   His mystery must be instressed, stressed;
> For I greet him the days I meet him, and bless when I under-
>   stand.   [p. 53]

This intensity does not lessen in any way the object's particularity. Rather, it makes it more striking, and in his poetry Hopkins tries to preserve this particularity in as immediate a way as possible. Like Rossetti, he attempts to portray the immediate sensuous impact of an object before the process of abstraction, but he tries to attain a much more complete particularization of poetry than Rossetti ever did. To make his poetry mime the shape of a single moment as it presents itself to sensation, he radically reshapes language itself.

In trying thus to reshape language, Hopkins has to struggle against its very nature. Words by definition denote classes of objects, acts, or qualities. They are common terms, not unique to single perceptions. They attempt to capture, conceptualize, and control individual experiences by placing them in general, hence communally understandable, categories. To counteract this generality, Hopkins tries to make words themselves into active, particular experiences rather than passive vehicles. In a discussion of what the word is, Hopkins concludes it is neither the thing referred to nor the response called up in the reader's mind, but "the expression, *uttering* of the idea in the mind. That idea itself has its two terms, the image (of sight or sound or *scapes* of the other senses), which is in fact physical and a refined energy accenting the nerves, a world to oneself, an inchoate word, and secondly the conception" (*J*, p. 125). He conceives of words as concrete, active forces that like objects carry within them the potential for creating a physical response, "a refined energy accenting the nerves." By his extremely unconventional use of words and by his dislocation of syntax, Hopkins makes language struggle to realize itself, to push itself out of the lassitude of generality, to maintain precision and particularity. And in the very act of imagination, a language particular to the act generates itself.

Of course, full particularity of language is impossible. In the *Essay Concerning Human Understanding*, Locke proposes the possibility of a completely particular language, in which each individual thing would have a distinct, peculiar name. He dismisses the possibility, however, not only because it is beyond the capacity of human memory to frame and retain distinct ideas of all the particular things it encounters but also because, even if it were not, such a language would prevent both communication and the process of categorization and relationship that constitutes human thought. Jorge Luis Borges has written a story called "Funes the Memorious," about a man who had a perfect memory for every detail he had ever perceived. Funes remembered not only every leaf of every tree of every wood but also every one of the times he had perceived or imagined it. He once had projected a completely particular language analogous to the one Locke postulates but discarded it as too general, too ambiguous. Not only was it difficult for him to comprehend that the generic symbol *dog* embraces so many different individuals, but it bothered him that the dog at 3:14 (seen from the side) should have the same name as the dog at 3:15 (seen from the front). The life of Funes shows the impossibility of an existence in which man could perceive things only in their full particularity. He would be immobilized by his memories, choked by the intolerably precise flood of sensations that rush upon him each moment, incapable of thought.

Without following the example of Funes, many modern philosophers and writers make a differentiation between our bodily sensations, which are particular and concrete, and the categories of language, which submerge the particular in the general and the abstract, and see reality not in the category but in the physical experience. Bergson's concept of intuition and its relationship to our habitual understanding of ourselves and the world is one of the principle modern philosophical treatments of this problem and one which tries to under-

stand the consequences for literature of the distance between
language and intuitive experience. Bergson sees literature as
trying to capture our primary intuitional experience of reality.
To do this the writer must disrupt the conventional categories
of language and see through them to the original experience.
To be completely true to this experience, Bergson asserts,
"new words would have to be coined, new ideas would have
to be created, but this would no longer be communicating
something, it would not be writing. Yet the writer will attempt
to realize the unrealizable." [14] T. E. Hulme, a disciple of Bergson and the philosopher associated with the imagist movement, created a poetic designed to attain this linguistic originality. He defines poetry as "a compromise for a language of
intuition which would hand over sensations bodily." "It always endeavours to arrest you, and to make you continuously
see a physical thing, to prevent you gliding through an abstract
process." [15] To create poetry that makes the reader see in this
way, Hulme asserts, poets must constantly invent fresh epi-
thets and metaphors. The bizarre metaphors of imagist poetry
result from this effort to startle the reader from old associations so that he can freshly experience a particular vision
through the poet's eyes.

    In a way similar to that called for by Hulme, Hopkins con-
tinually creates bizarre images.

The world is charged with the grandeur of God.
   It will flame out, like shining from shook foil;
   It gathers to a greatness, like the ooze of oil
Crushed.   [p. 66]

Nothing is so beautiful as Spring—
When weeds, in wheels, shoot long and lovely and lush;
Thrush's eggs look little low heavens . . .   [p. 67]

so some great stormfowl, whenever he has walked his while

The thunder-purple seabeach plumèd purple-of-thunder,
If a wuthering of his palmy snow-pinions scatter a colossal
  smile
Off him, but meaning motion fans fresh our wits with wonder.
                                                    [p. 80]

The strangeness of Hopkins's images immediately recalls the
metaphysical poets, but Hopkins uses this strangeness to very
different effect. The metaphysical poets use bizarre images to
make the reader perceive new intellectual relationships.
Donne's compasses, for example, don't make you see the
lovers in any physical way, but create an emblem that makes
you better understand the dynamics of their love. Donne uses
the bizarreness of the image to involve you in the perception
of an intellectual complexity. But the most striking thing
about Hopkins's images is not their intellectual but their
visual complexity. Their understanding often depends upon
and even has as its end the visualization of a physical fact.
The image of the smile ending "Henry Purcell" makes you
remember the way a bird's flight shows the color of its under-
wings. To understand the image of weeds growing in wheels
from "Spring," you must remember how weeds in fact grow
in early spring. Because Hopkins's emblem book is the natural
world, his poetry insists that the reader begin to understand
spiritual truths with the simple act of seeing. The images that
begin "God's Grandeur"—flaming out like shook foil, gathering to greatness like the ooze of oil crushed—are both images
of energy renewing itself under pressure, but the strangeness
of the images involves you as fully in their actual visualization,
their physical perception, as in the intellectual perception of
their meaning. Geoffrey Hartman has written that Hopkins's
poetry "is first an expression of sense experience and wants
at first to be taken as such." [16] The way Hopkins constructs
images demonstrates this fact. Like his poem about the chapel
at Oxford, all his metaphors make you go through the act of
seeing in order to catch the peculiar angle of his vision.
  Hopkins does not rely only upon startling metaphors to

make his poetry approach the act of particular perception. He is more radical than the imagists, even approaching Bergson's demand for new words in his transformation of each unit of language to mime the movement of particular perception as closely as possible. He counteracts the generalizing tendency of words by creating compounds that capture the distinctiveness of an object or experience. In words such as "wet-fresh," "much-thick," "wild-worst-Best," "couple-colour," "dare-gale," "foam-fleece," "very-violet-sweet," "fall-gold," Hopkins creates a unique fusion of qualities that crystallizes the particular essence of a moment of perception. Although these compounds still consist of one general conception delimited by another, they evade conventional linguistic categories in a way that enables Hopkins to suggest the moment a viewer immediately responds to an object when each of the parts of that response exists in its most primitive form. The mind perceives by recognizing or naming qualities upon which it only afterward imposes syntactically correct sentence structures. The use of coordinating conjunctions or the substitution of synonyms that unite the qualities is the result of a process of revision that separates the idea from the act of experiencing it. The compounding of words dramatizes the moment of immediate response, when each part of the response still preserves its peculiar emphasis, independence, and energy, while the hyphens fuse the qualities into a single perception. They force the reader to understand the words as a new, particular unit rather than as old, general categories under which to classify the object, as saying wet and fresh, or wild and worst and best, would do.[17] Hopkins in fact uses hyphens between words that are syntactically complete without them, such as "dappled-with-damson," "rarest-veined," "beauty-in-the-ghost," in order to transform the words into units that are fusions of qualities unique to the object, so that the act of naming becomes a particularizing experience.

Hopkins's transformation of parts of speech—his use of nouns as adjectives ("dooms-day dazzle," "shock night"), adjectives as nouns ("the past-prayer"), or verbs as nouns ("the hurl," "the achieve")—has much the same effect. For Hopkins, at the first stages of perception we recognize qualities or concepts with complete indifference to logical relationships or grammatical distinctions. Afterward, the mind arranges them in syntactically coherent form, but the initial experience is a simple juxtaposition of concepts that can be verbs or nouns or adjectives. Hopkins's transposition of parts of speech preserves the effect of this initial juxtaposition.

Hopkins also makes language more particular to the moment of apprehension through his dislocation of syntax. By this dislocation Hopkins can place the dominant characteristic or recognition of the perception first, so that the phrase reflects the order of imaginative apprehension. Take, for example, the beginning of "The Windhover":

> I caught this morning morning's minion, king-
> dom of daylight's dauphin, dapple-dawn-drawn
> Falcon in his riding
> Of the rolling level underneath him steady air . . .
>
> [p. 69]

In the phrase "underneath him steady," the direction of the perception or glance—underneath him—comes first, as it does in the act of realization, while the qualifying word "steady" comes second, followed by the noun. Normal syntax would require "the air that was steady underneath him," necessitating a revision of the order of perception and thus distancing it from reality. Furthermore, the placement of the noun *air* after all its modifiers allows the line to have a complete but different meaning when you stop at any point in its reading, because the adjectives that ultimately modify air can be seen as independent objects of the preposition *of*. The line can read "in his riding of the rolling," "in his riding of the rolling level," "in his riding of the rolling level underneath him," "in his riding of the rolling level underneath him steady," and finally, "in his riding of the rolling level underneath him steady air." By a word order that imitates the order of perception, in attaching different impulses to each other seemingly without a preconceived syntactic structure, Hopkins makes the sentence change meaning as it is read in exactly the way perception changes as it happens.

Another technique Hopkins uses is the omission of syntactical ligatures like pronouns, prepositions, and conjunctions. These parts of speech are generally used in the reformulation of immediate perceptions as more logical successions. By omitting the prepositions in phrases such as "the dearest freshness deep down things," "fastened me flesh," "thrush's eggs look little low heavens," Hopkins succeeds in imitating the quick associations we make upon perceiving objects, the immediate, nonanalytical apprehension of many elements at once. Likewise, Hopkins seldom uses coordinating conjunctions, and when he does use them he makes them merely signs of the continuation of thought, almost vocalic ellisions showing the increasing energy of his mind, not logical equivalency. He often begins the sestet of a sonnet, for example, with *and*. The sestet of "God's Grandeur" begins "And for all this, nature is never spent"; that of "Hurrahing in Harvest," "And the azurous hills are his world-wielding shoulder."

The way Hopkins creates series of nouns and adjectives further illustrates the immediate process of the imagination. In the opening description of the windhover, for example, each image seems to generate the next by an associative logic of sound and meaning. "Morning" produces "morning's minion," which produces in turn its symmetrical double, "kingdom of daylight's dauphin." The alliteration of the last two *d*'s of this phrase spins forth "dapple-dawn-drawn," which continues the idea of morning. The first line of adjectives in "Spelt from Sibyl's Leaves" illustrates this process of associative logic even more clearly.

> Earnest, earthless, equal, attuneable, | vaulty,
>   voluminous, . . . stupendous
> Evening strains to be tíme's vást | womb-of-all,
>   home-of-all, hearse-of-all night.   [p. 97]

The "er" sound of "earnest" generates "earthless"; "equal" alliterates once again. "Equal" produces by association "attuneable." "Vaulty" starts a second movement: "voluminous" both expands the sense of vastness and alliterates. "Stupendous" echoes the "u" sound and the idea of hugeness. The series of adjectives appears to be forming itself without premeditation. It expresses as far as possible the process by which an idea develops when first experienced. It begins by stating the idea in the first form that occurs; the second word is determined by the state in which the mind finds itself after the first has been spoken, and so on throughout the chain. Description is a fructifying, spawning, self-multiplying process, which generates its own particular form independent from and often in tension with the discursive movement of the poem. The method of advance from word to word is not logical; there is in fact a logical pause as the poet attempts to capture the shape of his perceptions. The only progress is one toward more vivid apprehension, an upward spiral, like that of the windhover, of the mind as it rises with the energy of its conception and views its subject from different levels.

By this kind of logical pause, Hopkins creates a tension between the hovering of the imagination over its subject and the linear discursive progress of a poem's statement. The adjectives describing the air underneath the windhover, for example—rolling, level, underneath him steady—require a suspension of logic until the poet apprehends all the aspects of the air. Phrases like "the achieve of, the mastery of the thing," or, from "The Wreck of the Deutschland," "the midriff astrain with leaning of, laced with fire of stress," or "finger of a tender, of, O of a feathery delicacy" suspend their grammatical completion in order to attain a more vivid imaginative realization. Hopkins's technique imitates the movement of the mind: it states a perception in one form, in the process of that statement realizes a more exact or slightly different form of the same perception, and so restates it, as in the phrase in "The Starlight Night," "the grey lawns cold where gold, where quickgold lies." By making this hovering movement of the descriptive imagination run in counterpoint with the logical movement of discursive statement, Hopkins makes his poetry mime the way a single perception generates its own direction.

The homophones and internal rhymes of Hopkins's series further add to our feeling that language is in the process of being generated. The likeness of sound makes it seem as if words are being formed from a primordial vocalic slime. The patterns of sound association that often guide the sequence of words create a sense of a particular language being formed from chaos by the imposition of different articulations upon a single sound, rather than the usual effect of the manipulation of an accepted set of symbols. The language seems in the process of emerging from its medium, much like a sculpture from its rock. The act of imaginative realization seems physically to create from unarticulated sound a particular language unique to that moment of perception.

Hopkins once wrote to Robert Bridges, "But as air, melody, is what strikes me most of all in music and design in painting, so design, pattern or what I am in the habit of calling 'inscape' is what I above all aim at in poetry." [18] Hopkins seeks to give each of his poems an individual distinctiveness, an inscape, equal to that of the objects he is describing. To do this, he has to proceed by the dislocations and disjunctions I have discussed, because language is general by nature, and only by wresting it from its conventional form can it be particularized. Hopkins's stylization is not an arbitrary one, however. In fact, he condemns the pursuit of an individually distinctive style for its own sake. "A horrible thing has happened to me," Hopkins wrote in a letter in 1864, "I have begun to *doubt* Tennyson." [19] He calls Tennyson's style "Parnassian," by which he means "that language which genius speaks as fitted to its exaltation, and place among other genius, but does not sing . . . in its flights." In short, it is the grand style adapted as a characteristic idiom, almost a mannerism. The fault Hopkins finds with the Parnassian style is its absence of inspiration. It is not in the highest sense poetry, he states, because "it does not require the mood of mind in which the poetry of inspiration is written." It is only the poet's habitual mode of speaking, and does not express the energy of his mind seeking the truth, because it does not require and consequently cannot dramatize the activity of the mind in the effort of imagination. It is poetry divorced from the central impetus of poetry, and therefore cannot touch the reader. Hopkins opposes Parnassian language to the language of inspiration, which communicates the abnormal mental acuteness, the stress and action of the brain in the process of creation. The poetry of inspiration conveys the shape of an imaginative apprehension as it strikes the mind, and Hopkins's stylizations of language all spring from an effort to mime that shape as closely as possible. He tries to get behind the discursive form of a thought to the texture of its immediate sensation, and his distinctiveness results not merely from personal eccentricity but, more importantly, from his effort to make the very form of language reflect that texture.

Hopkins creates his peculiar rhetoric to accommodate his vision of particular objects. The majority of Hopkins's poems consist of efforts, similar to those in his journals, to apprehend the inscapes of objects or scenes.

Towery city and branchy between towers;
Cuckoo-echoing, bell swarmèd, lark-charmèd, rook-racked,
    river rounded;

[p. 79]

Hard to hurdle arms, with a broth of goldish flue
Breathed round; the rack of ribs; the scooped flank, lank
Rope-over thigh; knee-nave; and barrelled shank—
    Head and foot, shoulder and shank—
By a grey eye's heed steered well, one crew, fall to;

[p. 104]

Cloud-puffball, torn tufts, tossed pillows | flaunt forth, then
    chevy on an air-
built thoroughfare: heaven-roysterers, in gay-gangs | they
    throng; they glitter in marches.
Down roughcast, down dazzling whitewash, | wherever an elm
    arches,
Shivelights and shadowtackle in long | lashes lace, lance, and
    pair.

[p. 105]

The particularity to which we have seen varying degrees of sensibility in the poetry of Tennyson, Rossetti, and Browning becomes for Hopkins the form of all perception, the primary mode of all knowledge. All generalization derives from concrete sensuous apprehension and thus is a step removed from our closest perception of reality. Hopkins's theory of knowledge approximates that of modern empiricists and reflects the way modern epistemology has reversed classical priorities by seeing truth in particulars experienced sensually rather than universals apprehended rationally, but Hopkins found theological support for his theory of knowledge in Duns Scotus, whom Hopkins names "of realty the rarest-veined unraveller." According to the Scotist theory of knowledge,

> every distinct act of knowing which takes in the adapted world of habit and practical necessity, has been preceded by a first act wherein sense and intellect are one, a confused intuition of Nature as a living whole, though the effect of the senses is to contract this intuition to a particular 'glimpse,' which is called the 'species specialissima.' Ordinarily, no sooner has the glimpse occurred than conation enters in and by abstraction adapts knowledge to suit needs. But if the first act is dwelt on to the exclusion of succeeding abstraction, then you can feel, see, hear or somehow experience the Nature which is yours and all creation's.[20]

The act of sensuous particular apprehension is the origin of all of our knowledge and our closest contact with the being of creation and of God. It is this primary apprehension, in which objects appear in their most immediate reality, that Hopkins tries to recreate in his poetry.

In reading Hopkins's poetry together with his journals, however, we surprisingly find a more precise observation of minute natural detail in his journals than in his poems. His poetry seems less particular in its use of detail than both his own notebooks and the other poets I have discussed. It contains few images as minute as Rossetti's woodspurge or Browning's beetles on an orange cup. The reason stems from the

fact that particularity in Hopkins's poetry is located not just
in the natural details observed but also in the act of apprehension. It is not principally sensitivity to detail but the
structure of the imaginative act that is the subject of his
poetry. Hopkins's poetry tries to change our sense of how we
see, and he places our focus on the act of apprehension principally by his use of language and metaphor rather than by
a use of minute detail.

Hopkins's conception of knowledge contains a remarkable
parallel to the thought of another Victorian convert to Ca-
tholicism, Cardinal Newman. In the *Grammar of Assent,*
which Hopkins in fact proposed editing,[21] Newman differentiates two kinds of assent, notional and real. Notional assent
is assent to propositions in which one or both terms are nouns
standing for what is abstract and general. Real assent is assent
to propositions in which the terms are nouns standing for
things external to us, unit, and individual. Of the two modes
of apprehending and assenting to propositions, the real is the
stronger, the more vivid and forcible, because "intellectual
ideas cannot compete in effectiveness with the experience of
concrete facts." *Real* may be understood as a philosophically
neutral term, but for Newman it quickly comes to connote
the human and the imaginatively rich, whereas notional comes
to suggest the dehumanizing, impoverishing, and falsifying.

> let units come first, and (so called) universals second; let
> universals minister to units, not units be sacrificed to
> universals. John, Richard, and Robert are individual
> things, independent, incommunicable. We may find some
> kind of common measure between them, and we may give
> it the name of man, man as such, the typical man, the
> *auto-anthropos.* We are justified in so doing, and in be-
> stowing on it what we consider a definition. But we think
> we may go on to impose our definition on the whole race,
> and to every member of it, to the thousand Johns, Rich-
> ards, and Roberts who are found in it. No; each of them
> is what he is, in spite of it. Not any one of them is man,

as such, or coincides with the *auto-anthropos*. . . . There is no such thing as stereotyped humanity; it must ever be a vague, bodiless idea, because the concrete units from which it is formed are independent realities.

With John and Richard

each is himself, and nothing else, and, though, regarded abstractly, the two may fairly be said to have something in common, (viz., that abstract sameness which does not exist at all,) yet strictly speaking, they have nothing in common, for each of them has a vested interest in all that he himself is; and, moreover, what seems to be common in the two, becomes in fact so uncommon, so *sui simile*, in their respective individualities . . . that, instead of saying, as logicians say, that the two men differ only in number, we ought, I repeat, rather to say that they differ from each other in all that they are, in identity, in incommunicability, in personality.

The abstracting faculty makes man into "the logarithm of his true self" in which shape he is worked "with the ease and satisfaction of logarithms." Likewise, abstract notions dilute and starve propositions about the concrete so that they become "little more intelligible than the beauties of a prospect to the shortsighted, or the music of a great master to a listener who has no ear."[22] Like Hopkins, Newman believes the primary source of our knowledge and the foundation of our most powerful beliefs lie in particular experience. In their assertion of the value of concrete sensuous experience, Hopkins and Newman resemble Rossetti and Pater. This coincidence of aesthetic and religious thought in the belief in the primacy of particular sensuous apprehension perhaps explains why the century's aesthetes so often seem priests manqués and its priests frustrated poets.

The importance placed on the sensuality and particularity of experience makes the act of sight, as Hartman observes, a moral responsibility, since moral and religious meaning do not belatedly disclose themselves to reason but are given in the very act of perception.[23] Hopkins always find in a particular perception an intuition of the reality of Christ or God. In the following passage from his journal, for example, he combines a botanically precise description of the bluebell with an intuitive realization of the beauty of Christ.

> I do not think I have ever seen anything more beautiful than the bluebell I have been looking at. I know the beauty of our Lord by it. Its inscape is mixed of strength and grace, like an ash tree. The head is strongly drawn over backwards and arched down like a cutwater drawing itself back from the line of the keel. The lines of the bell strike and overlie this, rayed but not symmetrically, some lie parallel. They look steely against the paper, the shades lying between the bells and behind the cockled petal-ends and nursing up the precision of their distinctness, the petal-ends themselves being delicately lit. Then there is the straightness of the trumpets in the bells softened by the slight entasis and by the square play of the mouth. One bell, the lowest, some way detached and carried on a longer footstalk, touched out with the tips of the petals an oval not like the rest in a plane perpendicular of the axis of the bell but a little atilt, and so with the square-in-rounding turns of the petals. [*J*, p. 199]

Hopkins's poems most often take the shape of an intensely sensuous perception of some natural object followed by the apprehension of the reality of God. "The Windhover" discovers the beauty of Christ's sacrifice in the flight of the bird. "The Starlight Night" finds that the stars house "Christ and his mother and all his hallows." "Spring" intuits the innocence of Eden and of children from the spring. "Pied Beauty" discovers God's changeless beauty from dappled things.

At first the movement of Hopkins's poems seems to resemble that of many Romantic poems, which ascend from the perception and contemplation of some natural object—a skylark, the west wind, a lamb, a wild flower—to the understanding of a transcendental reality, but the movement of Hopkins's poems is really quite different. The Romantic poets transform natural objects into symbols, but Hopkins's aggressive particularity implies a refusal to allow this transformation. Objects in his poems insist upon their individual identities. Hopkins does not make his wild flowers into symbols from which to ascend directly to heaven, but apprehends their most minute particularity and suddenly leaps to heaven. "The Windhover," for example, presents an intensely sensuous perception of a bird in soaring flight and in descent. Hopkins sees correspondences between the bird and Christ, but he realizes those correspondences not through idealization or abstraction but through an intense effort to apprehend the haeceitas, the physical particularity, of the bird before him. There is almost a disjunction between the naturalistic and the visionary levels of the poem which Hopkins bridges only by a thrust of sheer energy, an energy directed not up toward Christ but down toward a more sensuous apprehension of a particular object of His creation. Like Browning, Hopkins presents intensity as the force that makes possible the leap from the particular —not only, as I mentioned before, from a particular subjective impression to an authentic instress of the being of another object, but from the inscape of an object to the realization of the presence of Christ or God. Like Browning, his intensity takes the form of a heightened consciousness of particulars, but for Hopkins, this consciousness is an act of love both for God's creation and for "God's better beauty, grace." He sanctifies the good moment so that it becomes a sacrament, a physical tasting and drinking of the being of Christ.

To be sure, the possibility of Hopkins's leap of faith rests upon a transcendental assumption, but it is a strained transcendentalism. Nature no longer freely offers meaning in every landscape, as it did for Wordsworth. Man's vision of nature has grown more minute and detailed as nature's meaning has grown more remote. The transcendental eyeball has become myopic, and only an intense effort to apprehend the most minute particularity can lead man to the vision of any general truth. A vast gap separates the concrete phenomenon from any moral and religious insight, which can only be bridged by an intense emotional thrust toward the particular.

The writings of Ruskin perhaps contain the most striking example of this disjunction between the naturalistic and visionary modes of apprehension. The pages of precise scientific observation of cloud and land formations in *Modern Painters* together with its magnificent myth-making evidence his conviction, similar to Hopkins's, that man can best perceive nature's transcendental dimension by observing and recording natural phenomena in minutely accurate detail. The pages of his diary in fact read amazingly like those of Hopkins's journal, but a tension much greater than that in Hopkins exists between the two modes of apprehension in Ruskin. He follows his geologically detailed observations of rock formations with the transcendental myths "The Mountain Gloom" and "The Mountain Glory," but accepts their continuity without ever investigating the dynamics of the connection between them. This failure to provide a connection between modes of apprehension so seemingly incompatible produces the disjunction in his work.

Hopkins, like Browning, makes this dynamic connection the center of his poetic focus, but the leap beyond the particular nevertheless requires careful balance and strenuous intensity. The threat of isolation in the particular still hangs over Hopkins's world, not with regard to external objects but with regard to the self. In "The Probable Future of Metaphysics" he writes, "A form of atomism like a stiffness or sprain seems to hang upon and hamper our speculation: it is an overpowering, a disproportioned sense of personality" (*J*, p. 120). The "terrible" sonnets portray a self that cannot escape its own taste—that taste "more distinctive than the taste of ale or alum" but which has turned bitter.

> I am gall, I am heartburn. God's most deep decree
> Bitter would have me taste: my taste was me;
> Bones built in me, flesh filled, blood brimmed the curse.
>
> Selfyeast of spirit a dull dough sours. I see
> The lost are like this, and their scourge to be
> As I am mine, their sweating selves; but worse.

[p. 101]

Hopkins describes a world whose only reality is his own spirit feeding on itself. He lives within the continually twisting, self-reflective process of his own "tormented mind / With this tormented mind tormenting yet." In straining to reach God or his fellow man, he can only hear his heart grating on itself. His delight in his special distinctness has turned to a horror of solipsism. His vision of a world of particularity, like Browning's, holds within it the danger of morbidity. Like "Porphyria's Lover," like *Maud,* the "terrible" sonnets explore the burden of particularity of vision, the danger of an inflated fixation upon and imprisonment within the particular. While Tennyson and Browning distance the danger by using a mad speaker, however, Hopkins portrays it in the lyric voice so that it becomes the universal rather than the unusual condition. The irony and the curiosity that separate Browning from Porphyria's lover and the irony and morality that separate Tennyson from the hero of *Maud* are gone, leaving Hopkins to face directly the horror of a world in which all experience "is ringed round for each one by us by that thick wall of personality through which no real voice has ever pierced on its way to us, or from us to that which we can only conjecture to be without."

Epilogue

The poetry I have discussed in this book is one episode in the philosophical transformation that more than anything else distinguishes the modern from the classical and medieval world—the transformation from a world view that sees reality in a permanent order of universals to one that sees reality as an aggregate of individuals having particular experiences at particular times and places. This transformation results in a change of emphasis from classes to individuals, from eternity to the exigencies of time and space, from abstract thought to concrete sensuous apprehension, of which thought is but an element interwoven with the experience of sense. If universals are knowable at all in the modern world, they are knowable not through reason but through individual intuitions—a leap of faith, real assent, an epiphany, a good moment.

This philosophical change obviously involves important literary changes. Literature becomes less concerned with the apprehension of universals and the representation of ideals than the faithful recording of individual experience. The novel, of course, is the literary form that most completely reflects this philosophical change, and developments in the novel make it imitate more and more closely the form of lived experience. Virginia Woolf, for example, directs the following address to the modern novelist:

> Examine for a moment an ordinary mind on an ordinary day. The mind receives a myriad impressions—trivial, fantastic, evanescent, or engraved with the sharpness of steel. From all sides they come, an incessant shower of innumerable atoms . . .
> Let us record the atoms as they fall upon the mind in

the order in which they fall, let us trace the pattern, disconnected and incoherent in appearance, which each sight
or incendent scores upon the consciousness.[1]

But poetry is not without its changes too, and Rossetti,
Browning, and Hopkins are among the first to try to create a
poetry of lived experience. Different as they are in so many
respects, they are alike in their belief that reality lies not in
types but in particulars. Consequently, they try to change our
sense of the location of reality, our understanding of the way
we see. In doing so, they must overcome the resistance not
only of an artistic tradition but also of a language that distances and generalizes immediate experience. Rossetti's fleshliness, Browning's eavesdropping and his imitation of the
contortions and complexities of lived speech and thought,
Hopkins's strenuous fracturing of language are all attempts to
get at the point of experience as it is experienced, attempts
to create what Wallace Stevens calls "the poem of pure reality."
Yet this dependence upon naked particulars for truth is extremely vulnerable. Disclosure of meaning is not guaranteed
as it is with an a priori system of ideal forms. The fortuitous-
ness, the neutrality of phenomena constantly threaten to make
perception barren. The labyrinthine impenetrability of Robbe-
Grillet's purely phenomenal world, the immobility and the
failure to make connections of a Funes stand as constant possibilities once man admits the particularity of all phenomena.
As Wallace Stevens writes in "The Course of a Particular,"
the cry of leaves that do not transcend themselves is a cry
that concerns no one at all.
The twentieth century has solved this problem of the bar-
renness of mere particulars by a renewed assertion, such as we
find in Wallace Stevens, of the mind's role in constructing a
reality, which admits both the necessity and the personal relativity of universals. What made the Victorian predicament so
desperate was the fact that the Victorians wanted to find a
source of universals that was external to the self at the same
time that they were convinced of the subjectivity of experi-

ence. Browning and Hopkins resolved this problem by the creation of a dynamic of intensity. By sheer energy of perception, man brings about a moment's revelation of general truth, of eternity, of God.

Many writers of the twentieth century—James Joyce and Virginia Woolf are good examples—find what revelations experience offers in momentary visions, as do Hopkins and Browning, but such visions only provide a sudden radiance to daily reality. They no longer transcend the particular in an intuition of absolute truth as the Victorians worked so strenuously to do. They can only give it a momentary personal coherence, beauty—some might say love.

Yet the route to Joyce's epiphany runs from Wordsworth through Rossetti, Browning, and Hopkins, and it is they who give the personal, sensuous revelation of reality the Romantics sought its precariousness and its need for intensity. Their visions are far from secure. The leap from a system of assured correspondences to the observation of a world of particulars admits the possibility that the universe is not divine but arbitrary, and the only proof of revelation that remains is the intensity of personal experience.

Notes

Introduction

1 *On the Art of Poetry,* trans. Ingram Bywater (Oxford, 1959), p. 43.

2 For the most thorough modern discussion of the problem, see William K. Wimsatt, Jr., "The Structure of the 'Concrete Universal' in Literature," *PMLA* 62 (1947) : 262–80.

3 *Rasselas, Poems and Selected Prose,* ed. Bertrand H. Bronson, pp. 527–28.

4 *Laughter: An Essay on the Meaning of the Comic,* p. 161.

5 *The First and Second Discourses,* ed. Roger D. Masters, pp. 124–25.

6 Scott Elledge, ed., *Eighteenth Century Critical Essays,* 1 : 295–96.

7 *The Two Sources of Morality and Religion,* trans. R. Ashley Audra and Cloudesley Brereton, p. 242.

8 *The Collected Poetry of W. H. Auden* (New York, 1945), p. 267.

9 *The Literary Works of Sir Joshua Reynolds,* ed. Henry William Beechy, 2 : 132.

10 See William H. Youngren, "Generality, Science, and Poetic Language in the Restoration," *ELH* 35 (1968) : 186; also, William K. Wimsatt, Jr., and Cleanth Brooks, "The Neo-Classic Universal: Samuel Johnson," *Literary Criticism: A Short History,* pp. 314–35.

11 *Discourses on Art,* ed. Robert R. Wark, p. 45.

12 *Literary Works,* 2 : 135.

13 *Characteristics of Men, Manners, Opinions, Times,* quoted in Elledge, 1 : 174.

14 Elledge, 2 : 577.

15 Scott Elledge, "The Background and Development in English Criticism of the Theories of Generality and Particularity," *PMLA* 62 (1947) : 147–82.

16 See Ian Watt's discussion of the relationship of the philosophical tradition of realism and the form of the novel in *The Rise of the Novel,* pp. 9–34.

17 See Martin Price, "The Picturesque Moment," *From Sensibility to Romanticism*, ed. Frederick W. Hilles and Harold Bloom (New York, 1965), pp. 259–92.
18 *Lives of the English Poets*, 2 : 440.
19 *An Essay on the Genius and Writings of Pope*, 1 : 48.
20 *Biographia Literaria*, 2 : 33.
21 *The Poetical Works of William Wordsworth*, ed. E. de Selincourt, 2 : 394–95.
22 "On Certain Inconsistencies in Sir Joshua Reynolds' Discourses," *Collected Works* 6 : 132.
23 See *Works*, 4 : 332.
24 *The Friend*, ed. Barbara E. Rooke, 1 : 457.
25 "Coleridge," *Works*, 5 : 67.
26 For an account of this attempt see Zelda Boyd, "What the Poet Sees: A Study of the Aesthetic Theories of Mill, Carlyle, Ruskin, and Arnold."

Chapter One

1 J. Cuming Walters, *Tennyson: Poet, Philosopher, Idealist*, p. 252.
2 All quotations from Tennyson's poetry in my text are from *The Poems of Tennyson*, ed. Christopher Ricks (London, 1969).
3 "Tennyson's Poems," *Early Essays*, ed. J. W. M. Gibbs (London, 1897), pp. 242, 254.
4 See Valerie Pitt, *Tennyson Laureate*, p. 26; Humphrey House, "Tennyson and the Spirit of the Age," *All in Due Time*, p. 129. Some writers, however, still explain the microscopic observation of detail in Tennyson's poetry solely by his nearsightedness. "Part of Tennyson's fortune as a popular poet lay in his nearsightedness, which, by forcing him to examine natural objects such as flowers and leaves more closely than did most persons, enabled him to describe them in exceptionally fresh and faithful terms and thus to win his readers' admiration for his 'truth to nature'" (Richard D. Altick, *Victorian People and Ideas*, p. 274).
5 *Planet News* (San Francisco, 1968), pp. 141, 142.
6 *On Obsession: A Clinical and Methodological Study.*
7 Charles Tennyson, *Alfred Tennyson*, p. 484.
8 "Patterns of Morbidity: Repetition in Tennyson's Poetry," *The Major Victorian Poets: Reconsideration*, ed. Isobel Armstrong. pp. 30, 33–34.

9 Hallam Tennyson, *Tennyson: A Memoir*, 1 : 396.
10 New York, 1911, p. 33.
11 Boston, 1969, pp. 239–40.
12 In "Lucretius Among the Victorians" (*Victorian Studies* 16, no. 3 [1973] : 329–48), Frank M. Turner shows the way scientific and religious writers used Lucretius as a vehicle to carry on the debate about atomism and scientific materialism.
13 *The Central Self*, pp. 166–20.
14 Hallam Tennyson, 1 : 317.
15 *The Letters of Matthew Arnold to Arthur Hugh Clough*, ed. Howard Foster Lowry p. 97.
16 *English Poetic Theory: 1825–1865*, p. 153.
17 "Poetry with Reference to Aristotle's *Poetics*," *Essays Critical and Historical*, 1 : 9–10.
18 All quotations from Rossetti's poetry in my text are from *The Works of Dante Gabriel Rossetti*, ed. William M. Rossetti (London, 1911).
19 William Michael Rossetti, *Dante Gabriel Rossetti: His Family Letters with a Memoir*, p. 411.
20 "Rossetti," *Works*, 5 : 206; "The School of Giorgione," *Works*, 1 : 138.
21 See, for example, Harold L. Weatherby, "Problems of Form and Content in the Poetry of Dante Gabriel Rossetti," *Victorian Poetry* 2 (1964) : 11–19.
22 "Rossetti's Significant Details," *Victorian Poetry* 7 (1969) : 44.
23 *Works*, 5 : 211.
24 Berkeley, 1942.
25 "A Future for the Novel," *For a New Novel: Essays on Fiction*, pp. 15–24.
26 *Elizabethan and Metaphysical Imagery*. In her criticism of Eliot, Tuve distinguishes Renaissance and modern conceptions of the relationship between image, idea, and experience in poetry.
27 *Works*, 5 : 209.
28 *Against Interpretation and Other Essays*, pp. 13–23.
29 "Rossetti," *Works*, 5 : 207.
30 Sontag, p. 23.
31 *Victorian Poetry and Poetics*, ed. Walter E. Houghton and G. Robert Stange, p. 840.
32 *Letters of Dante Gabriel Rossetti*, ed. Oswald Doughty 1 : 46.
33 See *Letters of Dante Gabriel Rossetti*, ed. Oswald Doughty,

2 : 671–72; and T. Hall Caine, *Recollections of Rossetti*, p. 81.

34 Quoted in Hugh Kenner, *The Invisible Poet: T. S. Eliot* (New York, 1959), p. 152.

35 *Pre-Raphaelite Painters*, p. 13.

36 See, for example, Weatherby.

37 Herbert Sussman, "Hunt, Ruskin, and 'The Scapegoat,'" *Victorian Studies* 12 (1968) : 84.

38 William Holman Hunt, *Pre-Raphaelitism and the Pre-Raphaelite Brotherhood*, 1 : 147–50, 349.

39 "The Pictures of the Season," *Blackwood's Magazine* 68 (1850) : 82.

40 Quoted in A. Paul Oppé, "Art," *Early Victorian England 1830–1865*, 2 : 162.

41 "Old Lamps for New Ones," *Household Words* 1 (1850) : 266.

42 "The Art of England," *Works*, 33 : 288.

43 *Art and Visual Perception*, pp. 106–07.

44 See Humphrey House, "Pre-Raphaelite Poetry" in *All in Due Time* for a similar explanation of Pre-Raphaelite medievalism. House links its sacramentalism to the revival of sacramental doctrine in the Oxford movement.

45 Sussman, p. 85. Also see Ruskin, 14 : 65.

46 *Modern Painters, Works*, 3 : 186.

47 *Modern Painters, Works*, 6 : 30. See also 7 : 233, where he criticizes the Pre-Raphaelites for avoiding subjects expressing vastness, space, and mass and for fastening on "confined, broken, sharp forms" like furze, fern, reeds, straw, stubble or dead leaves. They show a mode of choice proceeding from "petulant sympathy" with local and immediately visible interests or sorrows without regarding their consequences.

48 Hunt, 1 : 350–51.

49 Quoted by Ironside, p. 24.

50 Ruskin, 12 : 334.

51 Quoted by Ironside, p. 24n.

52 "Are the Victorians Coming Back?" *All in Due Time*, p. 93.

Chapter Two

1 *The Letters of Matthew Arnold to Arthur Hugh Clough*, p. 97.

2 All quotations from the poetry of Browning in my text are from *The Poetical Works of Browning*, ed. Horace E. Scudder (Boston, 1895).

3 *Robert Browning,* pp. 246–56; see also William O. Raymond's discussion of this passage in " 'The Jeweled Bow': A Study of Browning's Imagery and Humanism," *The Infinite Moment and Other Essays in Robert Browning,* pp. 211–12.

4 "Wordsworth, Tennyson, and Browning; or, Pure, Ornate, and Grotesque Art in English Poetry," *Literary Studies,* 2 : 305–51.

5 Ibid., p. 338.

6 See Wolfgang Kayser, *The Grotesque in Art and Literature,* pp. 184–85. Kayser defines the grotesque as the estranged world, the world gone out of control, which forces us to face the central void of our existence. He emphasizes almost exclusively the terrifying tone of the grotesque, by dwelling largely on twentieth-century examples of its use. See also Mikhail Bakhtin's *Rabelais and His World* (Cambridge, Mass., 1968), which takes issue with the emphasis of Kayser's definition.

7 *Robert Browning,* p. 150. Chesterton also identifies the grotesque with the energy of the particular. He writes that the grotesque results from "the energy which takes its own forms and goes its own way" (p. 149).

8 See Robert Jay Lifton, "Protean Man," *Partisan Review* 35, no. 1 (Winter, 1968) : 13–27; and "Woman as Knower: Some Psychohistorical Perspectives," *The Woman in America,* ed. Robert Jay Lifton, pp. 36–37.

9 *The Disappearance of God,* p. 100.

10 See Lifton, cited above.

11 *Middlemarch,* ed. Gordon S. Haight (Boston, 1956), pp. 104–05.

12 *Disappearance of God,* pp. 136–37.

13 See Bagehot; Chesterton, pp. 133–59; Miller, pp. 87–90, 119–24, 135–36; Isobel Armstrong, "Browning and the 'Grotesque' Style," *Major Victorian Poets: Reconsiderations,* pp. 93–123.

14 Armstrong, p. 93.

15 Steward W. Holmes, "Browning: Semantic Stutterer," *PMLA* 60 (1945) : 231–55; and discussed by Miller, pp. 87–89. Holmes uses the phrase in a precise medical sense quite different from Miller's adaptation of it.

16 Armstrong, p. 96.

17 "Robert Browning's Pluralistic Universe: A Reading of *The Ring and the Book,*" *University of Toronto Quarterly* 31 (1961) : 20–41.

18 See *The Ring and the Book,* I, 1348–78.

19 In *The Poetry of Experience,* pp. 109–36, Robert Langbaum defines the relativism of *The Ring and the Book* in a similar way. He asserts that social and religious absolutes form barriers to understanding because the judgments of the poem are relative to its particular conditions and to the motives and quality of its characters. I disagree with Langbaum's use of the term "relativist," however, in its implication that the characters cannot perceive the absolute truth of the situation when in fact they can if they themselves have the right motives and if they sift through the mass of particular circumstances and motives involved in the case.

20 "Sir Walter Scott," *Works,* 29 : 77–78.

21 "Biography," *Works,* 28 : 47.

22 *Works,* 28 : 81.

23 "The French Revolution," *Early Essays,* pp. 275–76.

24 Ibid., p. 319.

25 Quoted by Maisie Ward, *Robert Browning and His World,* 2 : 45.

26 All quotations from the poetry of Hopkins in my text are from *The Poems of Gerard Manley Hopkins,* ed. W. H. Gardner and N. H. MacKenzie (London, 1967).

27 *The Journals and Papers of Gerard Manley Hopkins,* ed. Humphrey House, pp. 205–06. Hereafter cited as *J.*

28 *Works,* 3 : xxvi.

29 Ibid., p. 360.

30 *The Letters of Gerard Manley Hopkins to Robert Bridges,* ed. Claude Colleer Abbott, pp. 83–84, 170.

31 *Works,* 5 : 321.

32 *Works,* 7 : 207.

33 Quoted in *The Victorian Age,* ed. Robert Langbaum, p. 60.

34 *The English Novel: Form and Function,* pp. 126–27.

35 Miller, pp. 279–84.

Chapter Three

1 See Jerome Buckley, *The Triumph of Time.*

2 Hans Meyerhoff, *Time in Literature,* pp. 89–90.

3 Tennyson, *In Memoriam,* CXXIII.

4 See *The Renaissance,* p. ix.

5 *Robert Browning and Julia Wedgewood: A Broken Friendship As Revealed by their Letters,* ed. Richard Curle, p. 29.

6 *The Renaissance,* p. 150.

7 *The Letters of Robert Browning and Elizabeth Barrett Browning*, ed. Elvan Kintner, 1 : 17.
8 See John W. Tilton and R. Dale Tuttle, "A New Reading of 'Count Gismond,'" *Studies in Philology* 59 (1962) : 83–95; John V. Hagopian, "The Mask of Browning's 'Count Gismond,'" *Philological Quarterly* 40 (1961) : 153–55; Sister Marcella M. Holloway, "A Further Reading of 'Count Gismond,'" *Studies in Philology* 60 (1963) : 549–53.
9 See, for example, Robert Preyer, "Two Styles in the Verse of Robert Browning," *ELH* 32 (1965) : 78; Donald Davie, *Articulate Energy*, p. 74.
10 Isobel Armstrong, "Browning and the 'Grotesque' Style," in Armstrong, p. 110.
11 See particularly Paul F. Matthiesen, *Uproar in the Echo: The Existential Aesthetic of Browning's The Ring and the Book.*
12 See Walter E. Houghton, *The Victorian Frame of Mind*, pp. 291–97, for a discussion of this aspiration without an object.
13 *The Sermons and Devotional Writings of Gerard Manley Hopkins*, ed. Christopher Devlin, p. 123.
14 *The Two Sources of Morality and Religion*, p. 242.
15 *Speculations*, p. 134.
16 *The Unmediated Vision*, p. 53.
17 In his book, *Gerard Manley Hopkins*, pp. 107–20, W. A. M. Peters presents a similar argument for the frontal position of Hopkins's adjectives and adjective clauses. By this position he makes them fulfill a restrictive function, rather than a descriptive one, which emphasizes the unique being of the object rather than the categories to which it can belong.
18 *Letters to Robert Bridges*, p. 66.
19 *Further Letters of Gerard Manley Hopkins*, ed. Claude Colleer Abbott, p. 215.
20 Christopher Devlin, "Hopkins and Duns Scotus," *New Verse* 14 (April, 1935) : 13–14.
21 See *Further Letters*, p. 264, for Newman's reply to Hopkins's proposal. Newman refused the honor.
22 *An Essay in Aid of a Grammar of Assent*, p. 12, pp. 279–82, p. 31, p. 32.
23 *The Unmediated Vision*, p. 53.

Epilogue

1 *The Common Reader* (New York, 1953), pp. 154–55.

Bibliography

Abrams, M. H. *The Mirror and The Lamp: Romantic Theory and the Critical Tradition.* Chicago, 1947.

Altick, Richard D. *Victorian People and Ideas.* New York, 1973.

Armstrong, Isobel. "Browning and the 'Grotesque' Style." In *The Major Victorian Poets: Reconsiderations,* edited by Isobel Armstrong, pp. 93–123. London, 1969.

Arnheim, Rudolf. *Art and Visual Perception.* Berkeley, 1954.

Arnold, Matthew. *The Letters of Matthew Arnold to Arthur Hugh Clough.* Edited by Howard Foster Lowry. London, 1932.

Arnold, Matthew. *The Poems of Matthew Arnold.* Edited by Kenneth Allott. New York, 1965.

Arnold, Matthew. *Culture and Anarchy.* Edited by Ian Gregor. Indianapolis, Ind., 1971.

Bagehot, Walter. *Literary Studies.* 2 vols. London, 1944.

Ball, Patricia. *The Central Self.* London, 1968.

Bergson, Henri. *Laughter: An Essay on the Meaning of the Comic.* London, 1913.

Bergson, Henri. *The Two Sources of Morality and Religion.* Translated by R. Ashley Audra and Cloudesley Brereton. New York, 1935.

Boyd, Zelda. "What the Poet Sees: A Study of the Aesthetic Theories of Mill, Carlyle, Ruskin, and Arnold." Ph.D. dissertation, University of Michigan, 1971.

Browning, Robert. *The Poetical Works of Browning.* Edited by Horace E. Scudder. Boston, 1895.

Browning, Robert. *The Letters of Robert Browning and Elizabeth Barrett Browning.* Edited by Elvan Kintner. 2 vols. Cambridge, Mass., 1969.

Browning, Robert. *Robert Browning and Julia Wedgewood: A Broken Friendship as Revealed by Their Letters.* Edited by Richard Curle. New York, 1937.

Browning, Robert. "An Essay on Percy Bysshe Shelley." Edited by W. Tyas Harden. London, 1888.

Buckley, Jerome. *The Triumph of Time.* Cambridge, Mass., 1966.

Caine, T. Hall. *Recollections of Rossetti.* London, 1928.

Carlyle, Thomas. *Works.* 30 vols. London, 1899.

Chesterton, G. K. *Robert Browning.* London, 1926.

Coleridge, Samuel Taylor. *Biographia Literaria.* 2 vols. Oxford, 1962.

Coleridge, Samuel Taylor. *The Friend.* Edited by Barbara E. Rooke. 2 vols. Princeton, 1969.

Coleridge, Samuel Taylor. *Works.* 7 vols. New York, 1854.

Culler, A. Dwight. "The Darwinian Revolution and Literary Form." In *The Art of Victorian Prose,* edited by George Levine and William Madden, pp. 224–46. New York, 1968.

Davie, Donald. *Articulate Energy.* London, 1955.

Devane, W. C. *A Browning Handbook.* New York, 1955.

Devlin, Christopher. "Hopkins and Duns Scotus." *New Verse* 14 (April, 1935) : 12–17.

Dickens, Charles. "Old Lamps For New Ones." In *Household Words* 1 (1850) : 265–67.

Dodsworth, Martin. "Patterns of Morbidity: Repetition in Tennyson's Poetry." In *The Major Victorian Poets: Reconsiderations,* edited by Isobel Armstrong, pp. 7–34. London, 1969.

Doughty, Oswald. *A Victorian Romantic: Dante Gabriel Rossetti.* London, 1960.

Downes, David. *Victorian Portraits: Hopkins and Pater.* New York, 1965.

Elledge, Scott. "The Background and Development in English Criticism of the Theories of Generality and Particularity." *PMLA* 62 (1947) : 147–82.

Elledge, Scott, ed. *Eighteenth Century Critical Essays.* 2 vols. Ithaca, New York, 1961.

Fredeman, William E. *Pre-Raphaelitism: A Bibliocritical Study.* Cambridge, Mass., 1965.

Gardner, W. H. *Gerard Manley Hopkins (1884–1889): A Study of Poetic Idiosyncrasy in Relation to Poetic Tradition.* 2 vols. New Haven, 1948–49.

Hagopian, John V. "The Mask of Browning's 'Count Gismond.' " *Philological Quarterly* 40 (1961) : 153–55.

Hartman, Geoffrey H. *Hopkins: A Collection of Critical Essays.* Englewood Cliffs, New Jersey, 1966.

Hartman, Geoffrey H. *The Unmediated Vision.* New York, 1966.

Hazlitt, William H. *Collected Works.* 12 vols. London, 1903.

Herford, C. H. *Robert Browning.* Edinburgh, 1905.

Heuser, Alan. *The Shaping Vision of Gerard Manley Hopkins.* London, 1958.

Holloway, Sister Marcella M. "A Further Reading of 'Count Gismond.' " *Studies in Philology* 60 (1963) : 549–53.

Holmes, Stewart W. "Browning: Semantic Stutterer." *PMLA* 60 (1945) : 231–55.

Honan, Park. "Browning's Lyric Versification." In *Browning's Mind And Art,* edited by Clarence Tracy, pp. 82–99. Edinburgh, 1968.

Hopkins, Gerard Manley. *The Correspondence of Gerard Manley Hopkins and R. W. Dixon.* Edited by C. C. Abbott. London, 1935.

Hopkins, Gerard Manley. *Further Letters of Gerard Manley Hopkins.* Edited by C. C. Abbott. London, 1952.

Hopkins, Gerard Manley. *The Journals and Papers of Gerard Manley Hopkins.* Edited by Humphrey House and Graham Storey. London, 1959. Cited in the text as *J.*

Hopkins, Gerard Manley. *The Letters of Gerard Manley Hopkins to Robert Bridges.* Edited by C. C. Abbott. London, 1955.

Hopkins, Gerard Manley. *Poems of Gerard Manley Hopkins.* Edited by W. H. Gardner and N. H. MacKenzie. London, 1967.

Hopkins, Gerard Manley. *The Sermons and Devotional Writ-*

ings of Gerard Manley Hopkins. Edited by Christopher Devlin. London, 1959.

Hough, Graham. *The Last Romantics.* London, 1949.

Houghton, Walter E. *The Victorian Frame of Mind.* New Haven, 1963.

Houghton, Walter E. and Stange, G. Robert, eds. *Victorian Poetry and Poetics.* Cambridge, Mass., 1959.

House, Humphrey. *All in Due Time.* London, 1955.

Hulme, T. E. *Speculations.* New York, 1924.

Hunt, William Holman. *Pre-Raphaelitism and the Pre-Raphaelite Brotherhood.* 2 vols. London, 1905.

Ironside, Robin. *Pre-Raphaelite Painters.* New York, 1948.

Johnson, E. D. H. "Robert Browning's Pluralistic Universe: A Reading of *The Ring and the Book.*" *University of Toronto Quarterly* 31 (1961) : 20–41.

Johnson, Samuel. *Lives of the English Poets.* 2 vols. New York, 1857.

Johnson, Samuel. *Rasselas, Poems, and Selected Prose.* Edited by Bertrand H. Bronson. New York, 1966.

Kayser, Wolfgang. *The Grotesque in Art and Literature.* Bloomington, Ind., 1957.

Kermode, Frank. *The Sense of an Ending.* New York, 1968.

Killham, John. *Critical Essays on the Poetry of Tennyson.* New York, 1960.

Langbaum, Robert. *The Poetry of Experience.* New York, 1957.

Langbaum, Robert, ed. *The Victorian Age.* New York, 1967.

Lifton, Robert Jay. "Protean Man." *Partisan Review* 35, no. 1 (Winter, 1968) : 13–27.

Lifton, Robert Jay. "Woman as Knower: Some Psychohistorical Perspectives." In *The Woman in America,* edited by Robert Jay Lifton, pp. 27–51. Boston, 1967.

Lovejoy, Arthur O. *Essays in the History of Ideas.* Baltimore, 1948.

Matthiesen, Paul F. *Uproar in the Echo: The Existential Aesthetic of Browning's "The Ring and the Book."* Literary Monographs, Vol. 3. Madsion, Wis., 1971.

McGann, Jerome. "Rossetti's Significant Details." *Victorian Poetry*, 7 (1969) : 41–54.

Meyerhoff, Hans. *Time in Literature*. Berkeley, 1955.

Mill, John Stuart. *Early Essays*. London, 1897.

Miller, J. Hillis. *The Disappearance of God*. New York, 1965.

Newman, John Henry. *An Essay in Aid of a Grammar of Assent*. London, 1898.

Newman, John Henry. *Essays Critical and Historical*. 2 vols. London, 1872.

Oppé, A. Paul. "Art." In *Early Victorian England, 1830–1865*. London, 1934.

Pater, Walter. *Works*. 8 vols. London, 1900–01.

Peters, W. A. M. *Gerard Manley Hopkins: A Critical Essay Towards the Understanding of His Poetry*. London, 1948.

Pick, John. *Gerard Manley Hopkins: Priest and Poet*. New York, 1966.

Pitt, Valerie. *Tennyson Laureate*. Toronto, 1962.

Preyer, Robert. "Two Styles in the Verse of Robert Browning." *ELH* 32 (1965) : 62–84.

Price, Martin. "The Picturesque Moment." In *From Sensibility to Romanticism*, edited by Frederick W. Hilles and Harold Bloom, pp. 254–92. New York, 1965.

Raymond, William O. *The Infinite Moment and Other Essays in Robert Browning*. Toronto, 1965.

Reynolds, Graham. *Victorian Painting*. London, 1966.

Reynolds, Joshua. *Discourses on Art*. Edited by Robert R. Wark. New York, 1966.

Reynolds, Joshua. *The Literary Works of Sir Joshua Reynolds*. Edited by Henry William Beechy. 2 vols. London, 1846.

Robbe-Grillet, Alain. *For a New Novel: Essays on Fiction*. Translated by Richard Howard. New York, 1965.

Rossetti, Dante Gabriel. *Letters of Dante Gabriel Rossetti*. Edited by Oswald Doughty and John Robert Wahl. 4 vols. Oxford, 1965–67.

Rossetti, Dante Gabriel. *Letters of Dante Gabriel Rossetti*. Edited by William M. Rossetti. London, 1911.

Rossetti, William Michael. *Dante Gabriel Rossetti: His Family Letters with a Memoir.* Boston, 1895.

Rousseau, Jean Jacques. *The First and Second Discourses.* Edited by Roger D. Masters. New York, 1964.

Ruskin, John. *Works.* Edited by E. T. Cook and Alexander Wedderburn. 39 vols. London, 1903–12.

Sontag, Susan. *Against Interpretation and Other Essays.* New York, 1969.

Straus, Erwin. *On Obsession: A Clinical and Methodological Study.* New York, 1948.

Sussman, Herbert. "Hunt, Ruskin, and 'The Scapegoat.'" *Victorian Studies* 12 (1968) : 83–90.

Taylor, Houghton W. "Particular Character: An Early Phase of a Literary Evolution." *PMLA* 60 (1945) : 161–74.

Tennyson, Alfred. *The Poems of Tennyson.* Edited by Christopher Ricks. London, 1969.

Tennyson, Charles. *Alfred Tennyson.* New York, 1949.

Tennyson, Hallam. *Tennyson: A Memoir.* 2 vols. London, 1897.

Tilton, John W. and Tuttle, R. Dale. "A New Reading of 'Count Gismond.'" *Studies in Philology* 59 (1962) : 83–95.

Turner, Frank M. "Lucretius among the Victorians." *Victorian Studies* 16 (1973) : 329–48.

Tuve, Rosamund. *Elizabethan and Metaphysical Imagery.* Chicago, 1947.

Van Ghent, Dorothy. *The English Novel: Form and Function.* New York, 1961.

Walters, J. Cuming. *Tennyson: Poet, Philosopher, Idealist.* London, 1893.

Ward, Maisie. *Robert Browning and His World.* 2 vols. New York, 1967–69.

Warren, Alba. *English Poetic Theory: 1825–1865.* Princeton, 1950.

Warton, Joseph. *An Essay on the Genius and Writings of Pope.* 2 vols. London, 1782.

Watt, Ian. *The Rise of the Novel.* Berkeley, 1965.

Weatherby, Harold L. "Problems of Form and Content in the Poetry of Dante Gabriel Rossetti." *Victorian Poetry* 2 (1964) : 11–19.

Wimsatt, William K. and Brooks, Cleanth. *Literary Criticism: A Short History*. New York, 1957.

Wimsat, William K. "The Structure of the 'Concrete Universal' in Literature." *PMLA* 62 (1947) : 262–80.

Wordsworth, William. *The Poetical Works of William Wordsworth*. Edited by E. de Selincourt. 5 vols. Oxford, 1952.

Youngren, William H. "Generality, Science, and Poetic Language in the Restoration." *ELH* 35 (1968), 158–87.

Index

Aristotle, 1, 93

Arnheim, Rudolf, 58

Arnold, Matthew: interest in Lucretius, 32; attitude toward self-consciousness, 33–35; poetics of, 33–35, 49–50; attitude toward particularity, 34–35, 65–66, 93; *Culture and Anarchy*, 35; mentioned, 13, 78, 89, 104

Atomism, 32, 68–69, 99–102, 106

Auden, W. H., 4

Bagehot, Walter, 70 71

Bentham, Jeremy, 91–92, 110

Benthamism, 101

Bergson, Henri, 2, 3, 4, 134–35, 136

Blake, William, 10, 22, 46

Borges, Jorge Luis, 134

Brown, Ford Madox, 53, 61, 62

Browning, Robert: use of dramatic monologue, 12, 75–80, 85, 113; particularity in, 65–93, 111–27; relationship to Hopkins, 66, 103–04, 107, 132, 147,148–49; portrayal of nature, 66–74; and grotesque, 69, 71–74, 80–85; relationship to Romanticism, 74–76; grotesque style in, 80–85; pluralism in 85–87; judgment in, 87–89, 92–93; attitude toward history, 90, 92–93; the moment in, 111–23; relationship to Rossetti, 119; intensity in, 123–27; mentioned, 14, 35, 105, 143, 151, 152
—poems: "Abt Vogler," 122, 124; "Andrea del Sarto," 78; "Bishop Blougram's Apology," 13, 72; "The Bishop Orders His Tomb at St. Praxed's Church," 13, 79, 82, 113; "By the Fireside," 119–22, 123, 124, 126; "Caliban Upon Setebos," 13, 71, 73–74, 79–80, 89; "Cleon," 13; "Count Gismond," 117–19; "Cristina," 126–27; "The Englishman in Italy," 66–67, 68, 72–73, 121; "Fra Lippo Lippi," 78, 104, 113; *In a Balcony*, 85, 112; "The Last Ride Together," 112, 123, 127; "Meeting at Night," 113–14; "Mr. Sludge, 'the Medium,'" 71, 81–82, 89, 113; "My Last Duchess," 72; *Paracelsus*, 74–75, 85; "Parting at Morning," 114; *Pauline*, 74–75; *Pippa Passes*, 80–81, 86–87; "Porphyria's Lover," 71, 72, 89, 126–27, 149; *The Ring and the Book*, 83 84, 84 85, 87 88, 92 93, 158; "Saul," 124; "Sibrandus Schafnaburgensis," 67–68, 78; *Sordello*, 85; "Two in the Campagna," 114–17, 119, 122

Buchanan, Robert, 50

Carlyle, Thomas: attitude toward self-consciousness, 33, 34; *Sartor Resartus*, 33, 34, 76; attitude toward history, 89–92; criticism of *The Ring and the Book*, 92–93; mentioned, 13, 49–50, 104, 125

Chesterton, G. K., 71

Coleridge, Samuel, 1, 9, 10, 11, 13, 25, 110

Conrad, Joseph, 72, 127